Critic's Top 200 Albums

Compiled by Paul Gambaccini
with Susan Ready

With contributions from:
Loraine Alterman
Leonard J Beer
Chuck Blore
Geoffrey Cannon
Roy Carr
John Collis
Ray Connolly
Jonathan Cott
Robert Christgau
Cameron Crowe
Giovanni Dadomo
Robin Denselow
Chet Flippo
Ben Fong-Torres
Pete Frame
Simon Frith
Charlie Gillett
Bob Harris
Ron Jacobs
Clive James
Kid Jensen
Lenny Kaye
Murray The K
Dave Laing
Greil Marcus
Dave Marsh
Bruce Morrow
Hervé Muller
Scott Muni
Anne Nightingale
Mark P.
Tony Palmer
Tim Rice
Lisa Robinson
Robert Shelton
Dick Summer
John Tobler
Don Topping
Rosalie Trombley
Penny Valentine
Ed Ward
Chris Welch
Joel Whitburn
Richard Williams
Ellen Willis
Pete Wingfield
Ritchie Yorke

Omnibus Press
London/New York/Cologne/Sydney/Tokyo

This book is dedicated to Eric, Emmett, Jack, John, Throp and Hop.

Thanks to: Karen at Island, Maureen at Decca, Cherry and Pauline at Phonogram, Jane and Franco at WEA, Pauline at EMI, Lyndsey and Julia at CBS, Steve at Charmdale, everyone at 'Rock On', everyone at Harlequin, Dean Street, John Peel, Cliff White, Stella at Polydor and Diane at RCA.

Editor/Design Director:
Pearce Marchbank
Book design: Perry Neville

Exclusively distributed by Book Sales Limited, 78 Newman Street, London W1P 3LA
Quick Fox, 33 West 60th Street, New York, N.Y. 10023, USA.
Book Sales Pty. Limited, 27 Clarendon Street, Artarmon, Sydney, NSW 2064, Australia.
Music Sales Gmbh, Kölner Strasse 199, D-5000 Cologne 90, West Germany.

This book © Copyright 1978 Omnibus Press (A division of Book Sales Limited)

Introduction © Copyright 1978
Paul Gambaccini

All rights reserved. No part of this book may be reproduced in any form or by any electronic or mechanical means, including information storage and retrieval systems, without permission in writing from the publisher, except by a reviewer who may quote brief passages in a review.

Library of Congress
Catalogue No. 78-55565
ISBN 0.86001.494.0
UK Order No. OP 4035 1
US Order No. 250003

Printed in England by Lowe & Brydone Printers Limited, Thetford, Norfolk.

Album numbers: RCA Victor 2011, ABC S 590X, MGM Gas 131 and King 580 are not illustrated by their actual album sleeves as these were not available at time of going to press.

Introduction

By Paul Gambaccini

We rock buffs are crazy for lists. *American Top 40* is the most listened-to syndicated music programme in the world. The *Top Twenty* has the highest listening figures on the BBC. A listener-selected all-time top 100 is a surefire ratings winner on AM stations and is periodically a successful promotion for BBC Radio 1 and UK commercial stations. Even *Rolling Stone* and *New Musical Express* have printed ordered lists of rock's greatest hits.

If only for reasons of time and space, these surveys confine themselves to singles. A few hardy radio stations have invited their listeners to choose their favourite LPs, but even those have been unable to broadcast all of the records. Album lists are not as useful to radio stations as singles charts, and because a single song is an easier hook for press coverage than a group of songs, periodicals tend to emphasize hit 45s over LPs.

There has thus been a hole in literature of rock waiting to be filled, and as the seventies have gone by there have been more and more good reasons for filling it. A newcomer to rock music at the end of the decade faces an unprecedented challenge. Building a collection of the best albums available becomes an ever-expanding commitment as additional good records are added to the repertoire and the prices of deleted classics inflate. The neophyte needs a guide in choosing the core of his collection.

The fan who has rocked since the halcyon days of Presley and Berry or the chart coup d'etat by mid-sixties British groups may have a different problem. He feels he has seen it all, and wonders if there can be anything worth buying now that Buddy, Otis and Elvis have all left us. He needs a list to show him what he has missed on the long and winding road from Memphis.

Enter the experts, in this case nearly four dozen of them. Working in radio and music journalism on both sides of the Atlantic has given me a unique opportunity to hear the great disc jockeys and read the great rock critics of both the United States and Great Britain. It occurred to me that a cross-section of these men and women would select the most reliable ordered list of quality rock albums it is possible to obtain in our notoriously subjective world.

Regardless of how many times and no matter how violently we have disagreed with rock critics,

INTRODUCTION

we keep reading them anyway. We are mere human beings. Our judgment is fallible. We seek guidance for our taste and our expenditures. If the critics with column inch upon column inch at their disposal are human beings as well, we do not want to know. Without them we are at the mercy of record company advertising, the squeals of the loudest fans, and that inaccurate barometer of quality, reputation. Without rock critics, there would be anarchy in the browser bins.

I asked the people who appear

INTRODUCTION

in the second half of this book to list "the ten greatest rock albums of all-time, in order of preference." I did not attempt to define either "great" or "rock," since both words represent intangibles. Anyone who likes rock music knows what is and what is not rock, although he may choose to exclude a certain type of music on ethnic grounds. The range of albums chosen substantiates the assumption that it is the approach to music that an album is or is not "rock." Huey "Piano" Smith, the Wailers and Can co-exist with the Beatles, Stones, and Presley.

The diversity of this list does not mean it is bizarre in its upper reaches. Weighing the votes on a point system revealed basically unsurprising preferences for the Beatles, Rolling Stones and Dylan. But surprises do appear in two ways. Firstly, individuals respond to entertainment idiosyncratically as well as part of the herd, and some selections are rather unique favourites. In the bottom half of the two hundred the reader will find some amusingly personal choices.

The second surprise will be cultural. Britons may be shocked, for example, that so many Americans rated **Born to Run** highly. Unfamiliar with urban New York, they cannot fully appreciate the power and perceptiveness of Bruce Springsteen's work. Conversely, most Americans will surely be baffled by British votes for **The Clash**, a punk rock album not even released in the United States whose sensitivities, while equally urban, are of a different generation in different circumstances.

We provide a substantial amount of useful information with each entry, believing that many readers will be tempted to buy some of the albums they see. In the case of LPs whose track listings were altered for American release, we have given the more complete British listings.

Assembling the sleeves of two hundred albums for photographing was an exercise in logistical horror. For her role in this gruelling task Sue Ready deserves more than thanks, she deserves to never have to phone an oldies shop again in her life. Still, her lot would have been worse without the gracious assistance of Pete Frame, Mike Hawkes, John Peel, John Tobler, and Cliff White.

Readers puzzling over the absence of Peel from these pages may be curious to know that a few invited experts declined to participate, most pleading either laziness or a lack of expert judgment. The vast majority who replied did so with enthusiasm, and their personal choices appear in the second half of the book. If you have ever wondered what the deejay you have long respected listens to at home, or what that critic you have long resented actually likes, here is your chance to find out. I thank them all for participating in the spirit of the project, which is the same reason you've read this far. Read on, enjoy, and, if you want, disagree with somebody.

THE TOP 200 ALBUMS

Sgt. Pepper's Lonely Hearts Club Band
The Beatles

UK: Parlophone PMC 7027
US: Capitol 2653
Produced by George Martin
Published 1967

Sgt. Pepper's Lonely Hearts Club Band
A Little Help From My Friends
Lucy In The Sky With Diamonds
Getting Better
Fixing A Hole
She's Leaving Home
Being For The Benefit Of Mr. Kite!
Within You Without You
When I'm Sixty-Four
Lovely Rita
Good Morning, Good Morning
Sgt. Pepper's Lonely Hearts Club Band, Reprise
A Day In The Life

Chosen number one by Chris Welch:
"These boys were kings of the Big Beat Sound. Or put it another way, one was immediately impressed by the rushing flow of ideas, burst as from a pent up dam. The magical quality of the performance and production, in which time seemed suspended, caused the listener to join in some hallucinatory state, experienced by the musicians, producer and possibly even the studio tea lady. I sat in a somewhat inebriated state in an

THE TOP 200 ALBUMS

2

Blonde On Blonde
Bob Dylan

Indian restaurant recently, where this album was being used as a background. I almost shed tears at hearing it again, and in such circumstances."

Chosen number one by Ron Jacobs:
"Hard to rate these LP's in order, let alone list a mere ten — but, this one I had the pleasure of hearing and playing first (while Program Director at KHJ Los Angeles) and that experience gives this the sentimental edge."

Chosen number one by Murray The K:
"It represents a work synonymous with the era and the influence on all groups. It is a symbol of progression, growth and variety."

Chosen number one by Joel Whitburn:
"In 1964, the music world was expanded nearly double with the explosion of The Beatles in America. **Sgt. Pepper's** *nearly doubled our musical visions again in 1967. Can any rock fan around the world ever forget their feelings upon first hearing this monumental album in the summer of '67.* **Sgt. Pepper's** *was then and still is one of the greatest listening experiences for the rock ear."*

UK: CBS 66012
US: Columbia 2-841
Produced by Bob Johnston
Published 1966

Rainy Day Women Nos. 12 & 35
Pledging My Time
Visions Of Johanna
One Of Us Must Know
I Want You
Memphis Blues Again
Leopard-Skin Pill-Box Hat
Just Like A Woman
Most Likely You Go Your Way
   And I'll Go Mine
Temporary Like Achilles
Absolutely Sweet Marie
4th Time Around
Obviously 5 Believers
Sad Eyed Lady Of The Lowlands

Chosen number one by Roy Carr:
"I have already bled white, two copies of this album and I'm currently working on a third!"

Chosen number one by Lenny Kaye:
"Time speeded up compressed cinemascope of images, totally rich in profusion. Anything can be abstracted from the universe of 'Sad Eyed Lady Of The Lowlands'. My desert island album."

Chosen number one by Robert Shelton:
"A classic burst of rock energy,

Bob Dylan (Columbia Archive)

THE TOP 200 ALBUMS

poetic language and searching sensibility. A double album that is geometrically witty, sad, bright, touching. Varied enough in mood to the point of being encyclopaedic. Belongs as much to the music of today as to the day before yesterday."

3

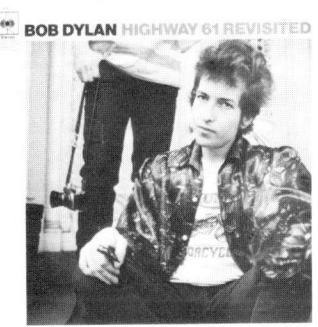

Highway 61 Revisited
Bob Dylan

UK: CBS 62572
US: Columbia 9189
Produced by Bob Johnston
Published 1965

Like A Rolling Stone
Tombstone Blues
It Takes A Lot To Laugh, It Takes A Train To Cry
From A Buick Six
Ballad Of A Thin Man
Queen Jane Approximately
Highway 61 Revisited
Just Like Tom Thumb's Blues
Desolation Row

Chosen number one by Simon Frith:
"Not because of what he says but because of the way he says

it. Dylan finally silenced all doubters and showed that the very things that had confined previous rock expression to three minute bursts — the monotony of dance-based rhythms, the banality of lyrics hemmed in by melodic and rhyming conventions — could become, if sustained, hypnotic and engrossing. Like all great inventors, Dylan didn't create anything new, just packaged it differently."

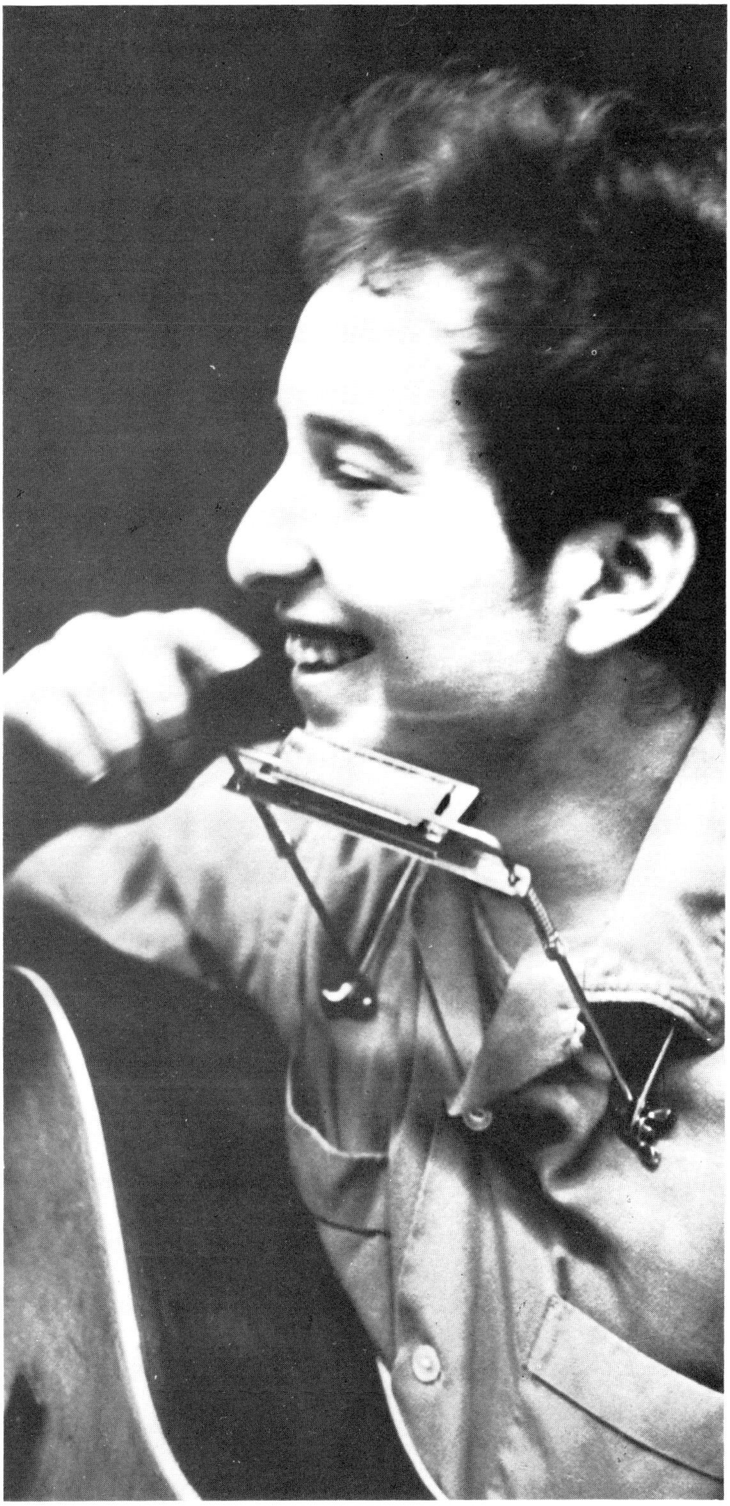

Bob Dylan (Columbia Archive)

THE TOP 200 ALBUMS

4

Astral Weeks
Van Morrison

UK: K46024
US: WAR 1768
Produced by Lewis Merenstein
Published 1968

Astral Weeks
Beside You
Sweet Thing
Cyprus Avenue
Young Lovers Do
Madame George
Ballerina
Slim Slow Slider

Chosen number one by Pete Frame:
"It just is. No explanation necessary."

Chosen number one by Kid Jensen:
"An LP although regularly played I never tire of. It creates rather than complements a mood at any time of day. It always reminds me of the golden days of '67/'68. A timeless work – beautiful!"

5

Rubber Soul
The Beatles

UK: Parlophone PMC 1267
US: Capitol 2442
Produced by George Martin
Published 1965

Drive My Car
Norwegian Wood
Up I Won't See Me

THE TOP 200 ALBUMS

Nowhere Man
Think For Yourself
The Word
Michelle
What Goes On
Girl
I'm Looking Through You
In My Life
Wait
If I Needed Someone
Run For Your Life

Chosen number one by Jonathan Cott.

6

Revolver
The Beatles

UK: EMI PCS 7009
US: Capitol 2576
Produced by George Martin
Published 1966

Taxman
Eleanor Rigby
I'm Only Sleeping
Love You To
Here, There and Everywhere
Yellow Submarine
She Said She Said
Good Day Sunshine
And Your Bird Can Sing
For No One
Dr. Robert
I Want To Tell You
Got To Get You Into My Life
Tomorrow Never Knows

John Lennon

Chosen number one by Dick Summer:
"**Revolver** defined the age and the music. 'Eleanor Rigby' was as powerful as Vatican II."

THE TOP 200 ALBUMS

Let It Bleed
The Rolling Stones

UK: SKL 5025
US: London 4
Produced by Jimmy Miller
Published 1969

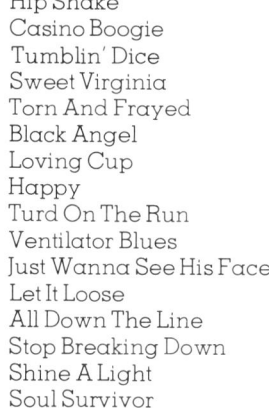

Hip Shake
Casino Boogie
Tumblin' Dice
Sweet Virginia
Torn And Frayed
Black Angel
Loving Cup
Happy
Turd On The Run
Ventilator Blues
Just Wanna See His Face
Let It Loose
All Down The Line
Stop Breaking Down
Shine A Light
Soul Survivor

Chosen number one by Robert Cristgau.

Exile On Main Street
Rolling Stones

UK: COC 69 100
US: Rolling Stones 2900
Produced by Jimmy Miller
Published 1972

Rocks Off
Rip This Joint

THE TOP 200 ALBUMS

9

Mick Jagger

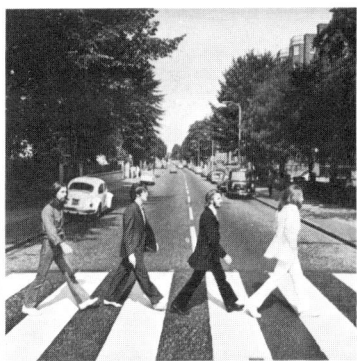

Abbey Road
The Beatles

UK: PCS 7088
US: Apple 383
Produced by George Martin
Published 1969

Come Together
Something
Maxwell's Silver Hammer
Oh! Darling
Octopus's Garden
I Want You (She's So Heavy)
Here Comes The Sun
Because
You Never Give Me Your Money
Sun King
Mean Mr Mustard
Polythene Pam
She Came In Through The Bathroom Window
Golden Slumbers
Carry That Weight
The End

Chosen number one by Robin Denselow:
"The freshest, most inventive, most jammed full of ideas and fine melodies, of all the Beatles'

Let It Bleed
Love In Vain
Midnight Rambler
Gimme Shelter
You Got The Silver
You Can't Always Get What You Want
Live With Me
Monkey Man
Country Honk

Chosen number one by Greil Marcus:
"**Let It Bleed** *is not only one of the most intelligent rock and roll albums ever made, but also one of the most visceral and exciting. It not only summed up its era as well as any recording has ever done, it has escaped its era, and sounds as direct and mysterious today as it did upon release in late 1969. It includes what may well be the greatest single rock and roll performance ('Gimme Shelter') plus some of the most surprising ('You Got The Silver,' 'You Can't Always Get What You Want').* **Let It Bleed** *is more than anyone could have expected from the Rolling Stones – more, in fact, than any fan could have hoped for. That kind of satisfaction is part of what rock and roll is all about."*
Also chosen number one by Ellen Willis.

THE TOP 200 ALBUMS

albums. My favourite, because of fond sixties associations, it still stands up as a great record."

Chosen number one by Leonard J Beer:
"Overpowering – especially to someone born in New York City – songwriting and production combination is masterful."

Chosen number one by Dave Marsh:
"A modern distillation, I think, of the entire rock & roll tradition – not just in terms of influences but also because of its spirit, and its use of the form, not to mention expressions of the crucial urban sensibility."

10

Born To Run
Bruce Springsteen

UK: CBS 69170
US: PC 33795
Produced by Bruce Springsteen, Jon Landau, and Mike Appel
Published 1975

Thunder Road
Tenth Avenue Freeze-Out
Night
Backstreets
Born To Run
She's The One
Meeting Across The River
Jungleland

11

The Sun Collection
Elvis Presley

UK: RCA HY 1001
US: RCA APM 1-1675
Produced by Sam Phillips
Published 1975

That's All Right (Mama)
Blue Moon Of Kentucky
I Don't Care If The Sun Don't Shine
Good Rockin' Tonight
Milkcow Blues Boogie
You're A Heartbreaker
I'm Left, You're Right, She's Gone
Baby, Let's Play House
Mystery Train
I Forgot To Remember To Forget
I Love You Because
Tryin' To Get To You
Blue Moon
I'll Never Let You Go
I Love You Because

12

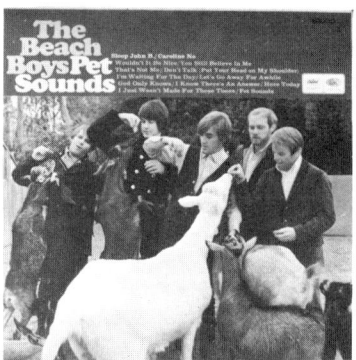

Pet Sounds
The Beach Boys

UK: EMI ST 2458
US: Capitol 2458
Produced by Brian Wilson
Published 1966

Wouldn't It Be Nice
You Still Believe In Me
That's Not Me
Don't Talk (Put Your Head On My Shoulder)
I'm Waiting For The Day
Let's Go Away For A While
Sloop John B
God Only Knows
I Know There's An Answer
Here Today

THE TOP 200 ALBUMS

I Just Wasn't Made For These Times
Pet Sounds
Caroline No

Chosen number one by Richard Williams:
*"Any comment I might offer on the merits of **Pet Sounds** would be too subjective to hold any value."*

13

Garth Hudson, The Band

The Band
The Band

UK: STAO 132
US: Capitol 132
Produced by The Band
Published 1969

Across The Great Divide
Raga Mama Rag
The Night They Drove Old Dixie Down
When You Awake
Up On Cripple Creek
Whispering Pines
Jemima Surrender
Rockin' Chair
Look Out Cleveland
Jawbone
The Unfaithful Servant
King Harvest (Has Surely Come)

14

The Velvet Underground And Nico

UK: Verve Super 2315 056
US: Verve 65008
Produced by Andy Warhol
Published 1967

Levon Helm, The Band

THE TOP 200 ALBUMS

Eric Clapton

THE TOP 200 ALBUMS

Sunday Morning
I'm Waiting For The Man
Femme Fatale
Venus In Furs
Run Run Run
All Tomorrow's Parties
Heroin
There She Goes Again
I'll Be Your Mirror
The Black Angel's Death Song
European Son

Chosen number one by
Lisa Robinson:
"It changed my life, what else?"

15

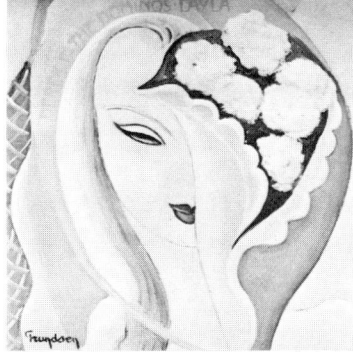

Layla And Other Assorted Love Songs
Derek & The Dominoes

UK: RSO Super 2671 110
US: ATCO 704
Executive Producer Tom Dowd
Produced and arranged by The Dominoes
Published 1971

I Looked Away
Bell Bottom Blues
Keep On Growing
Nobody Knows You When
    You're Down And Out
I Am Yours
Anyday
Key To The Highway
Tell The Truth
Why Does Love Got To Be So Sad
Have You Ever Loved A Woman
Little Wing
It's Too Late
Layla
Thorn Tree In The Garden

16

Forever Changes
Love

UK; Elektra K42015
US: Elektra 74013
Produced by Arthur Lee with Bruce Botnick
Published 1976

Alone Again Or
A House Is Not A Motel
And More Again
The Daily Planet
Old Man
The Red Telephone
Maybe The People Would Be
    The Times Or Between
    Clark And Hilldale
Live And Let Live
The Good Humour Man He Sees
    Everything Like This
Bummer In The Summer
You Set The Scene

Chosen number one by
Bob Harris:
"Released in 1967, some years ahead of its time. Production, arrangements, lyrical and musical content is first class throughout. One of those very rare albums which does not have one bad track. A classic recording and my favourite L.P. of all time."

Chosen number one by
Penny Valentine:
"You expect comments at a time like this? Eat your chicken soup and be nice to your mother. I am retiring in a nicotine haze."

Love (Rex Features)

THE TOP 200 ALBUMS

Jimi Hendrix

18

The Beatles
The Beatles

UK: PCS 7067-8
US: Apple 101
Produced by George Martin
Published 1968

3rd Stone From The Sun
Remember
Are You Experienced

17

Red House
Can You See Me
Love Or Confusion
I Don't Live Today
May This Be Love
Fire

Are You Experienced
Jimi Hendrix Experience

UK: Track 612001
US: Reprise 6261
Produced by Chas Chandler
Published 1976

Foxy Lady
Manic Depression

The Beatles

THE TOP 200 ALBUMS

Back In The U.S.S.R.
Dear Prudence
Glass Onion
Ob-La-Di, Ob-La-Da
Wild Honey Pie
The Continuing Story Of
   Bungalow Bill
While My Guitar Gently Weeps
Happiness Is A Warm Gun
Martha My Dear
I'm So Tired
Blackbird
Piggies
Rocky Raccoon Don't Pass Me By
Why Don't We Do It In The Road
I Will
Julia
Birthday
Yer Blues
Mother Nature's Son
Everybody's Got Something To
   Hide Except Me And My
   Monkey
Sexy Sadie
Helter Skelter
Long, Long, Long
Revolution 1
Honey Pie
Savoy Truffle
Cry Baby Cry
Revolution 9
Good Night

19

Who's Next
The Who

UK: Track 2408 102
US: Decca 79182

Roger Daltrey (Chalkie Davies)

Produced by The Who
Associate Producer Glyn Johns
Executive Producers Kit Lambert, Chris Stamp, Pete Cameron
Published 1971

Baba O'Riley
Bargain
Love Ain't For Keeping
My Wife
Song Is Over
Getting In Tune
Going Mobile
Behind Blue Eyes
Won't Get Fooled Again

THE TOP 200 ALBUMS

20

Legend
Buddy Holly

UK: CDMSP 802
US: Not released in USA
Produced by Norman Petty
Published 1957, 1958 & 1959 (compilation album)

It's So Easy
Tell Me How
Not Fade Away
I'm Looking For Someone To Love
That'll Be The Day
Think It Over
Maybe Baby
Oh Boy
Everyday
Listen To Me
Well... All Right
I'm Gonna Love You Too
Early In The Morning
Words of Love
Peggy Sue
Heartbeat
Rave On
Bo Diddley
Midnight Shift
Brown Eyed Handsome Man
Rock Around With Ollie Vee
Love's Made A Fool Of You Baby
I Don't Care
Reminiscing
Wishing
Moondreams
True Love Ways
Raining In My Heart
It Doesn't Matter Anymore
Peggy Sue Got Married
Learning The Game
Love Is Strange
What To Do

Chosen number one by Chet Flippo:
"The basis of all modern rock & roll is contained in this collection".

21

Tapestry
Carole King

UK: SP 77009
US: Ode 77009
Produced by Lou Adler
Published 1971

I Feel The Earth Move
So Far Away
It's Too Late
Home Again
Beautiful
Way Over Yonder
You've Got A Friend
Where You Lead
Will You Love Me Tomorrow
Smackwater Jack
Tapestry
(You Make Me Feel Like) A Natural Woman

THE TOP 200 ALBUMS

22

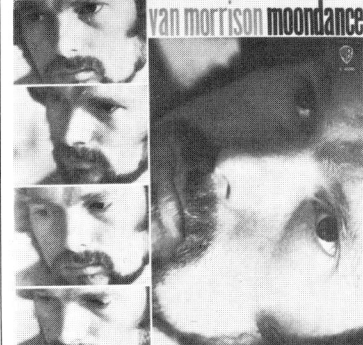

Moondance
Van Morrison

UK: K 46040
US: WB 1835
Produced by Van Morrison
Published 1970

Stoned Me
Moondance
Crazy Love
Caravan
Into The Mystic
Come Running
These Dreams Of You
Brand New Day
Everyone
Glad Tidings

23

Otis Blue
Otis Redding

UK: Atlantic K 40003
US: Volt 412
Session supervised by Tom Dowd
Published 1966

Ole Man Trouble
Respect
Change Gonna Come
Down In The Valley
I've Been Loving You Too Long
Shake
My Girl
Wonderful World

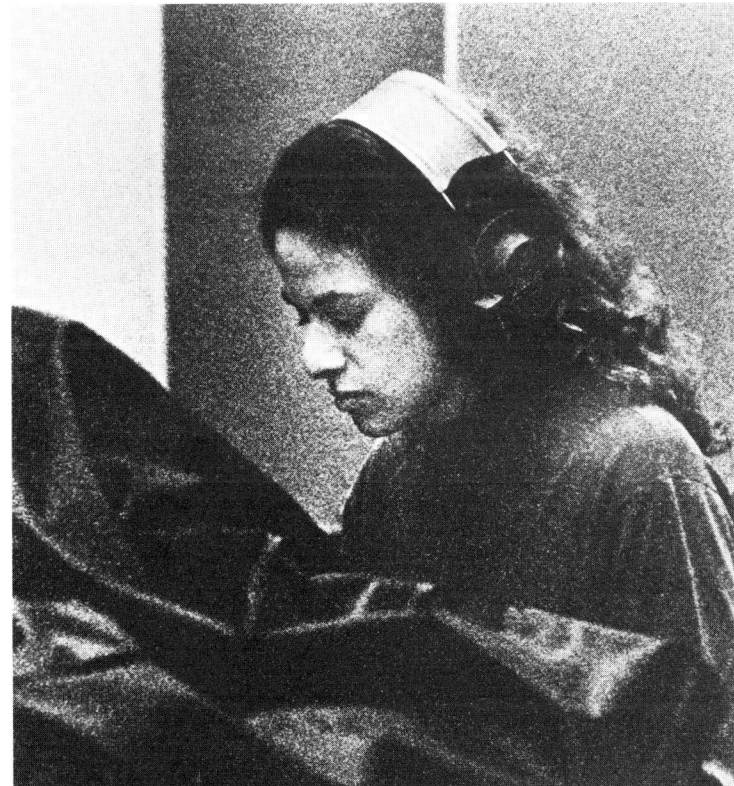

THE TOP 200 ALBUMS

Rock Me Baby
Satisfaction
You Don't Miss Your Water

24

The Clash
The Clash

UK: CBS 8200
US: Not yet released in US
Produced by Nicky Foot
Published 1977

Janie Jones
Remote Control
I'm So Bored With The USA
White Riot
Hate & War
What's My Name
Deny
London's Burning
Career Opportunities
Cheat
Protex Blue
Police & Thieves
48 Hours
Garageland

Chosen number one by Giovanni Dadomo:
"Because anytime is 'all-time' and, there being no time like the present, there's nothing that excites and inspires me more than **The Clash**."

Chosen number one by Mark P:
"This album says more about real British life than The Beatles, Dylan and Hendrix rolled into one. **Blonde On Blonde** or **Sgt. Pepper's** will probably come top but **The Clash** is much more important."

25

Blood On The Tracks
Bob Dylan

UK: CBS 69097
US: Col. PC-33235
Produced by Bob Dylan
Published 1974

Tangled Up In Blue
Simple Twist Of Fate
You're A Big Girl Now
Idiot Wind
You're Gonna Make Me Lonesome When You Go
Meet Me In The Morning
Lily, Rosemary And The Jack Of Hearts
If You See Her, Say Hello
Shelter From The Storm
Buckets Of Rain

Chosen number one by Geoffrey Cannon:
"'Lily, Rosemary And The Jack Of Hearts'. The best of Dylan, and Dylan's the best."

26

The Harder They Come
Soundtrack from the film

THE TOP 200 ALBUMS

UK: Island ILPS 9202
US: MLPS 9202
Produced by various people
Published 1972

You Can Get It If You Really Want
Draw Your Brakes
Rivers Of Babylon
Many Rivers To Cross
Sweet And Dandy
The Harder They Come
Johnny Too Bad
Shanty Town
Pressure Drop
Sitting In Limbo
You Can Get It If You Really Want, Reprise
The Harder They Come, Reprise

Chosen number one by Charlie Gillett: "Comment is redundant – listen to it!"

27

Bringing It All Back Home
Bob Dylan

UK: CBS 62515
US: Col. PC-9128
Produced by Tom Wilson
Published 1965

Subterranean Homesick Blues
She Belongs To Me
Maggie's Farm
Love Minus Zero/No Limit
Outlaw Blues
On The Road Again
Bob Dylan's 115th Dream
Mr Tambourine Man
Gates Of Eden
Its Alright, Ma (I'm Only Bleeding)
It's All Over Now, Baby Blue

28

Imagine
John Lennon

UK: PAS 10004
US: Apple 3379
Produced by John, Yoko and Phil Spector
Published 1971

Imagine
Jealous Guy
Gimme Some Truth
Crippled Inside
It's So Hard
I Don't Wanna Be A Soldier
Oh Yoko
How
Oh My Love
How Do You Sleep

29

Led Zeppelin IV
Led Zeppelin

UK: Atlantic K 50008
US: Atlantic 7208
Produced by Jimmy Page
Published 1971

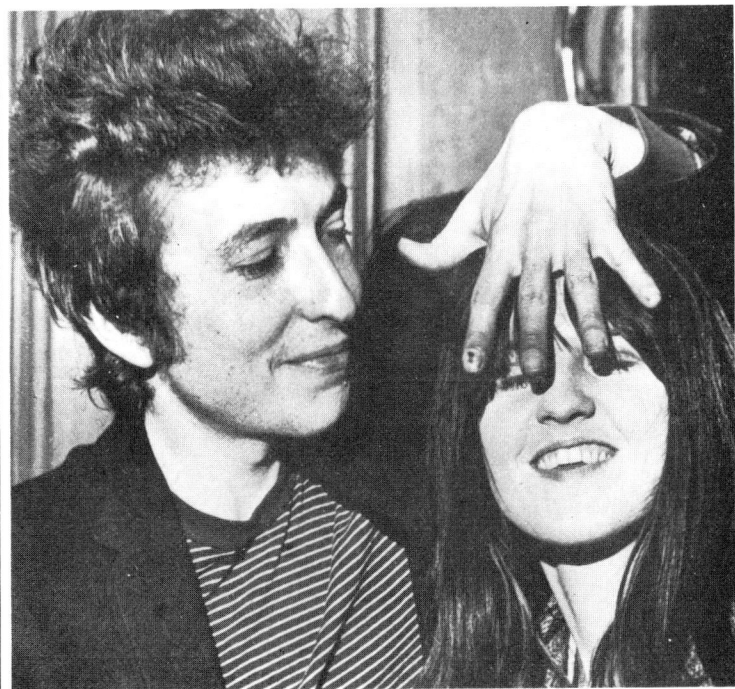

Bob Dylan & Cathy McGowan

THE TOP 200 ALBUMS

John Paul Jones, Led Zeppelin

31

My Generation
The Who

UK: LAT 8616
US: MCA 2-4068
Produced by Kit Lambert
Published 1965

Out In The Street
I Don't Mind
The Good's Gone
La-La-La-Lies
Much Too Much
My Generation
The Kids Alright
Please Please Please
It's Not True
I'm A Man
A Legal Matter
The Ox

Black Dog
Rock 'n' Roll
The Battle Of Evermore
Stairway To Heaven
Misty Mountain Top
Four Stick
Going To California
When The Levee Breaks

Waiting For My Man
Lisa Says
What Goes On
Sweet Jane
We're Gonna Have A Real Good Time Together
Femme Fatale
New Age
Rock And Roll
Beginning To See The Light
Ocean
Pale Blue Eyes
Heroin
Some Kinda Love
Over You
Sweet Bonnie Brown/It's Just Too Much
White Light/White Heat
I'll Be Your Mirror

30

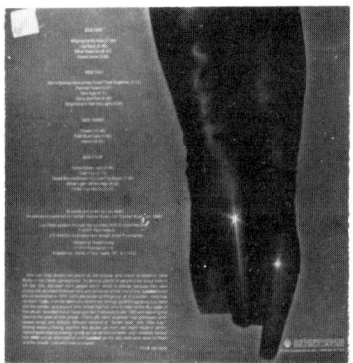

1969 Velvet Underground Live
The Velvet Underground

American release only
US: SRM-2-7504
Published 1974

The Who

THE TOP 200 ALBUMS

Art Garfunkel (Tom Sheehan)

Nobody's Fault But Mine
Hard To Handle
Thousand Miles Away
The Happy Song
Think About it
A Waste Of Time
Champagne & Wine
A Fool For You
Amen

34

32

There's A Doctor
Go To The Mirror
Tommy Can You Hear Me
Smash The Mirror
Sensation
Miracle Cure
Sally Simpson
I'm Free
Welcome
Tommy's Holiday Camp
We're Not Gonna Take It

33

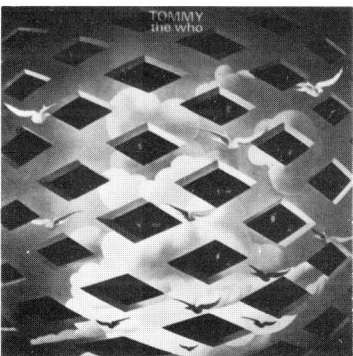

Tommy
The Who

UK: Track 2657 002
US: Decca 7205
Produced by Kit Lambert
Published 1969

Overture
It's A Boy
1921
Amazing Journey
Sparks
The Hawker
Christmas
Cousin Kevin
The Acid Queen
Underture
Do You Think It's Alright?
Fiddle About
Pinball Wizard

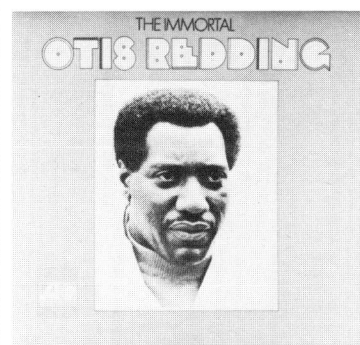

The Immortal Otis Redding
Otis Redding

UK: Atlantic 588113
US: Atco 252
Produced by Steve Cropper
Published 1968

I've Got Dreams To Remember
You Made A Man Out Of Me

Parsley, Sage, Rosemary and Thyme
Simon and Garfunkel

UK: CBS 62860
US: Columbia 9363
Produced by Paul Simon
Published 1966

Scarborough Fair/Canticle
Patterns
Cloudy
The Big Bright Green Pleasure
  Machine
The 59th Street Bridge Song
  (Feelin' Groovy)
The Dangling Conversation
Flowers Never Bend With The
  Rainfall
A Simple Desultory Philippic
  (Or How I was Robert
  McNamara'd Into
  Submission)
For Emily, Whenever I May
  Find Her
A Poem On The Underground
  Wall
7 O'Clock News/Silent Night

Chosen number one by Scott Muni.

THE TOP 200 ALBUMS

35

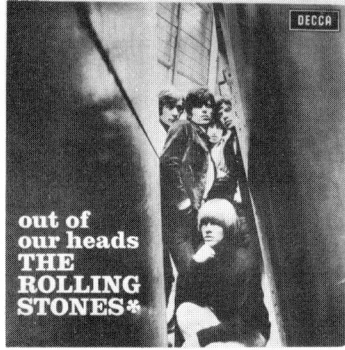

Out Of Our Heads
The Rolling Stones

UK: SKL 4733
US: London 429
Produced by Andrew Look Oldham
Published 1965

She Said Yeah
Mercy, Mercy
Hitch Hike
That's How Strong My Love Is
Good Times
Gotta Get Away
Talkin' Bout You
Cry To Me
Oh, Baby (we got a good thing going)
Heart Of Stone
The Under Assistant West Coast Promotion Man
I'm Free

36

California Bloodlines
John Stewart

UK: ST 203
US: Capitol 203
Produced by Nik Venet
Published 1969

California Bloodlines
Razor-back Woman
She Believes In Me
Omaha Rainbow
The Pirates Of Stone County Road
Shackles And Chains
Mother Country
Some Lonesome Picker
You Can't Look Back
Missouri Birds
July, You're A Woman
Never Goin' Back

37

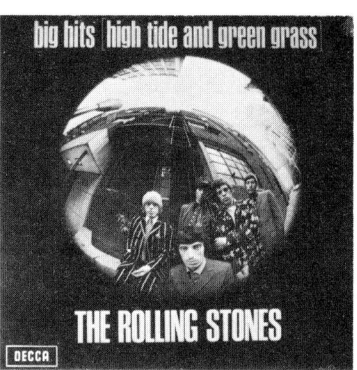

Big Hits (High Tide And Green Grass)
The Rolling Stones

UK: Decca TXS 101
US: London 1
Produced by Andrew Loog Oldham
Published 1966

Have You Seen Your Mother, Baby, Standing In The Shadow?
Paint It, Black
It's All Over Now
The Last Time
Heart Of Stone
Not Fade Away
Come On
(I Can't Get No) Satisfaction
Get Off Of My Cloud
As Tears Go By
19th Nervous Breakdown
Lady Jane
Time Is On My Side
Little Red Rooster

The Rolling Stones

THE TOP 200 ALBUMS

38

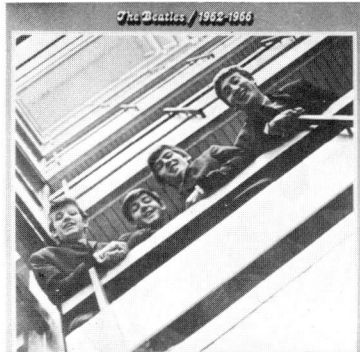

The Beatles 1962-1966
The Beatles

UK: PCSP 717
US: Cap. SKBO-3403
Produced by George Martin
Published 1973

Love Me Do
Please, Please Me
From Me To You
She Loves You
I Want To Hold Your Hand
All My Loving
Can't Buy Me Love
A Hard Day's Night
And I Love Her
Eight Days A Week
I Feel Fine
Ticket To Ride
Yesterday
Help!
You've Got To Hide Your Love Away
We Can Work It Out
Day Tripper
Drive My Car
Norwegian Wood (This Bird Has Flown)
Nowhere Man
Michelle
In My Life
Girl
Paperback Writer
Eleanor Rigby
Yellow Submarine

Chosen number one by Dave Laing:
"Because they came first and (with Dylan) made possible most of the nine which follow."

The Beach Boys

39

Endless Summer
The Beach Boys

UK: EA-ST 11307
US: Capitol SVBB 11307
Compilation Michael R. Ross
Published 1974

Surfin' Safari
Surfer Girl
Catch A Wave
The Warmth Of The Sun
Surfin' U.S.A.
Be True To Your School
Little Deuce Coupe
In My Room
Shut Down
Fun, Fun, Fun
I Get Around
Girls On The Beach
Wendy
Let Him Run Wild
Don't Worry Baby
California Girls
Girl Don't Tell Me
Help Me Rhonda
You're So Good To Me
All Summer Long

Chosen number one by Bruce Morrow:
"The Beach Boys are probably one of the most important American rock groups of all time. They have influenced several generations' music taste and their influence on today's music is quite obvious."

THE TOP 200 ALBUMS

Stevie Wonder

Knocks Me Off My Feet
Pastime Paradise
Summer Soft
Ordinary Pain
Isn't She Lovely
Joy Inside My Tears
Black Man
Ngiculela — Es Una Historia
I Am Singing
If It's Magic
As
Another Star

Chosen number one by Rosalie Trombley:
"Over two years in the making . . . it was worth the wait. This album is what the title suggests, music and a message for everyone of all ages. We in the 'Motor City' are very proud, continued success Stevie."

40

Chosen number one by Cameron Crowe:
"Somehow **After The Goldrush** held just the right combination of historical importance, magic and memories to come out on top for me. It was very close."

41

42

After The Goldrush
Neil Young

UK: Reprise K44088
US: Reprise 6383
Produced by Neil Young and David Briggs
Published 1972

Tell Me Why
After The Goldrush
Only Love Can Break Your Heart
Southern Man
Till The Morning Comes
Oh Lonesome Me
Don't Let It Bring You Down
Birds
When You Dance I Can Really Love
I Believe in You
Crippled Creek Ferry

Songs In The Key Of Life
Stevie Wonder

UK: Motown TMSP 6002
US: Tam. 13-340C2
Produced by Stevie Wonder
Published 1976

Love's In Need Of Love Today
Have A Talk With God
Village Ghetto Land
Confusion
Sir Duke
I Wish

Beggars Banquet
The Rolling Stones

UK: Decca SKL 4955
US: London 539
Produced by Jimmy Miller
Published 1968

Sympathy For The Devil
No Expectations
Dear Doctor
Parachute Woman
Jig-Saw Puzzle
Street Fighting Man
Prodigal Son
Stray Cat Blues
Factory Girl
Salt Of The Earth

THE TOP 200 ALBUMS

43

The Doors
The Doors

UK: Elektra K 42012
US: Elektra 74007
Produced by Paul A. Rothchild
Published 1976

Break On Through (To The Other Side)
Soul Kitchen
The Crystal Ship
Twentieth Century Fox
Alabama Song (Whisky Bar)
Light My Fire
Back Door Man
I Looked At You
End Of The Night
Take It As It Comes
The End

44

There Goes Rhymin' Simon
Paul Simon

UK: CBS 69035
US: Col. PC-32280
Produced by Paul Simon
Published 1973

Kodachrome
Tenderness
Take Me To The Mardi Gras
Something So Right
One Man's Ceiling Is Another Man's Floor
American Tune
Was A Sunny Day
Learn How To Fall
St. Judy's Comet
Loves Me Like A Rock

45

James Brown At The Apollo, Vol. 1
James Brown

UK: Polydor 2482 184
US: King 826
Live album
Published 1962

I'll Go Crazy
Try Me
Think
I Don't Mind
Lost Someone
Please, Please, Please
You've Got The Power
I Found Someone
Why Do You Do Me Like You Do
I Want You So Bad
I Love You Yes I Do
Why Does Everything Happen To Me
Bewildered
Please Don't Go
Night Train

Chosen number one by Pete Wingfield:
"At the time it was simply the most exciting music I had ever heard and fifteen years later it still takes some beating –

Paul Simon

THE TOP 200 ALBUMS

David Bowie (Mick Rock)

despite the use of 'canned' screams alongside the genuine variety. The most worn album in my collection."

46

Every Picture Tells a Story
Rod Stewart

UK: Mercury 6338 063
US: Mercury 609
Produced by Rod Stewart
Published 1971

Every Picture Tells A Story
Seems Like A Long Time
That's All Right
Tomorrow Is A Long Time
Maggie May
Mandolin Wind
(I Know) I'm Losing You
Reason To Believe

47

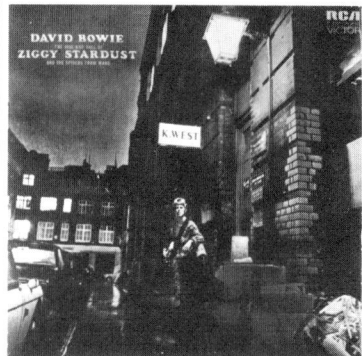

The Rise And Fall of Ziggy Stardust
David Bowie

UK: RCA Victor SF 8287
US: RCA Victor 4702
Produced by David Bowie and Ken Scott
Published 1972

Five Years
Soul Love
Moonage Daydream
Starman
It Ain't Easy
Lady Stardust
Star
Hang On To Yourself
Ziggy Stardust
Suffragette City
Rock 'n' Roll Suicide

48

Saint Dominic's Preview
Van Morrison

UK: Warner Bros. K 46172
US: Warner Bros. 2633
Produced by Van Morrison
Published 1972

Jackie Wilson Said (I'm In
    Heaven When You Smile)
Gypsy
I Will Be There
Listen To The Lion
Saint Dominic's Preview
Redwood Tree
Almost Independence Day

49

Frampton Comes Alive
Peter Frampton

THE TOP 200 ALBUMS

UK: A&M 63703
US: A&M 3703
Produced by Peter Frampton
Published 1975

Something's Happening
Doobie Wah
Show Me The Way
It's A Plain Shame
All I Want To Be (Is By Your Side)
Wind Of Change
Baby, I Love Your Way
I Wanna Go To The Sun
Penny For Your Thoughts
(I'll Give You) Money
Shine On
Jumping Jack Flash
Lines On My Face
Do You Feel Like We Do

51

Blood, Sweat And Tears
Blood, Sweat And Tears

UK: CBS 63504
US: Columbia 9720
Produced by James William Guercia
Published 1969

Variations On A Theme By Eric Satie
Smiling Phases
Sometimes In Winter
More And More
And When I Die
God Bless The Child
Spinning Wheel
You've Made Me So Very Happy
Blues Part 11
Variations On A Theme By Eric Satie, Reprise

52

Live At Leeds
The Who

50

With The Beatles
The Beatles

UK: Parlophone PCS 3045
US: Capitol 2047 (American title 'Meet The Beatles')
Produced by George Martin
Published 1963

It Won't Be Long
All I've Got To Do
All My Loving
Don't Bother Me
Little Child
Till There Was You
Please Mister Postman
Roll Over Beethoven
Hold Me Tight
You Really Got A Hold On Me
I Wanna Be Your Man
Devil In Her Heart
Not A Second Time
Money

Peter Frampton

THE TOP 200 ALBUMS

UK: Track 2406 001
US: Decca 79175
Live Album
Published 1970

Young Man
Substitute
Summer Time Blues
Shakin' All Over
My Generation
Magic Bus

53

We're Only In It For The Money
The Mothers Of Invention

UK: Verve Select 2317 034
US: Verve 5045
Produced by Frank Zappa
Published 1968

Are You Hung Up
Who Need The Peace Corps
Concentration Moon
Mom And Dad
Bow Tie Daddy
Harry, You're A Beast
What's The Ugliest Part Of Your Body
Absolutely Free
Flower Punk
Hot Poop
Nasal Retentive Calliope Music
Let's Make The Water Turn Black
The Idiot Bastard Son
Lonely Little Girl
Take Your Clothes Off When You Dance
What's The Ugliest Part Of Your Body (Reprise)
Mother People
The Chrome Plated Megaphone Of Destiny

54

Surf's Up
The Beach Boys

UK: Stateside SSL 10313
US: Reprise 6453
Produced by The Beach Boys
Published 1971

Don't Go Near The Water
Long Promised Road
Take A Load Off Your Feet
Disney Girl (1957)
Student Demonstration Time
Feel Flows
Lookin' At Tomorrow (A Welfare Song)
A Day In The Life Of A Tree
'Till I Die
Surf's Up

55

Meaty Beaty Big And Bouncy
The Who

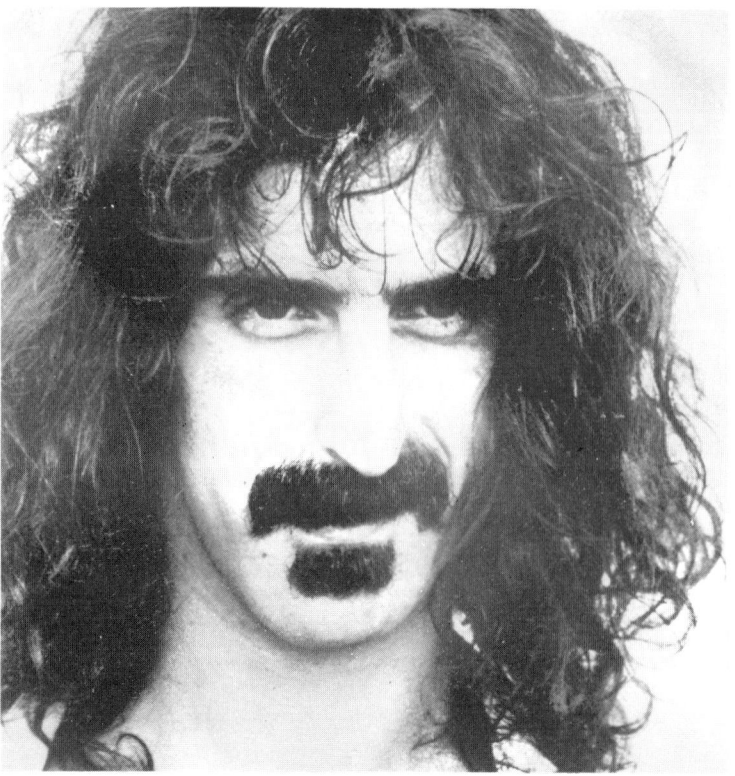

Frank Zappa

THE TOP 200 ALBUMS

UK: Track 2406 006
US: Decca 79184
Produced by Shel Talmy, Kit Lambert and The Who
Published 1971

I Can't Explain
The Kids Are Alright
Happy Jack
I Can See For Miles
Pictures Of Lily
My Generation
The Seeker
Anyway, Anyhow, Anywhere
Pinball Wizard
Legal Matter
Boris The Spider
Magic Bus
Substitute
I'm A Boy

56

Bob Dylan Greatest Hits
Bob Dylan

UK: CBS 62847
US: Columbia 9463
Produced by John Hammond, Tom Wilson, Bob Johnson
Published 1967

Blowin' In The Wind
It Ain't Me Babe
The Times They Are A-Changin'
Mr. Tambourine Man
She Belongs To Me
It's All Over Now Baby Blue
Subterranean Homesick Blues
One Of Us Must Know
Like A Rolling Stone
Just Like A Woman
Rainy Day Women Nos. 12 & 35
I Want You

57

Boz Scaggs
Boz Scaggs

UK: K 40419
US: Atlantic SD 8239
Produced by Boz Scaggs, Jann Wenner, Marlin Greene
Published 1969

I'm Easy
I'll Be Long Gone
Another Day
Now You're Gone
Finding Her
Look What I Got

Waiting For A Train
Loan Me A Dime
Sweet Release

58

And The Hits Just Keep On Comin'
Michael Nesmith

UK: Island ILPS 9439
US: Pac. 9439
Produced by Michael Nesmith
Published 1972

Tomorrow & Me
The Upside Of Good-Bye

THE TOP 200 ALBUMS

Lady Love
Listening
Two Different Roads
The Candidate
Different Drum
Harmony Constant
Keep On
Roll With The Flow

Chosen number one by John Tobler:
"*Apart from the fact that this is probably the least commercially successful album on anyone's list, and has only recently been released in Britain four years later, the lack of premeditation on the part of the artist, the sarcastic title and the extreme instrumental scarcity, the latter a quality only noticeable in comparison with every other album, have kept this a constant favourite since I first heard it.*"

59

Average White Band
Average White Band

UK: Atlantic K50058
US: 2-At 1002
Produced by Arif Mardin
Published 1974

You Got It
Got The Love
Pick Up The Pieces
Person To Person
Work To Do
Nothing You Can Do
Just Wanna Love You Tonight
Keepin' It To Myself

I Just Can't Give You Up
There's Always Someone Waiting

Chosen number one by Chuck Blore.

60

Chirping Crickets
Buddy Holly & The Crickets

UK: Coral CP 20
US: BL 54038
Produced by Norman Petty
Published 1957

That'll Be The Day
I'm Looking For Someone To Love
Oh Boy
You've Got Love
Maybe Baby
It's Too Late
Tell Me How
Send Me Some Lovin'
An Empty Cup (And A Broken Date)
Last Night
Rock Me My Baby
Not Fade Away

Chosen number one by John Collis:
"*The other eight artists in my 'Top Ten' are heroes, but Buddy Holly is more. Fortunately his genius and the vital collaboration of such as Jerry Allison and Norman Petty, are demonstrable on the 'real' album as well as on the many permutation records that followed. Holly did more than combine country and blues, as did many others; he invented pop music.*"

Average White Band

THE TOP 200 ALBUMS

61

Dedicated To You
The Five Royales

US: King 580 (deleted)
This is a very rare album, I think unreleased in the U.K. It was issued some time in the early 50's.

Think
Someone Made You For Me
Just As I Am
Don't Be Ashamed
Come On And Save Me
I'd Better Make A Move
Dedicated To The One I Love
Right Around The Corner
Say It
Messin' Up
Tears Of Joy
30 Second Lover

Chosen number one by Ed Ward:
"Even though I didn't discover it until 15 years after it was cut, this album epitomizes my idea of rock and roll. Well-written songs, hot guitar playing (by whom? Lonnie Mack? Lowman Pauling?), great harmony singing, and the kind of production that means the finished product will still be rough around the edges. Anyway, as a critic, I'm supposed to deal with the obscure as well as the prominent and popular. If I could, I'd mail a copy of this rare album to just about everybody who wanted to know where I was coming from."

62

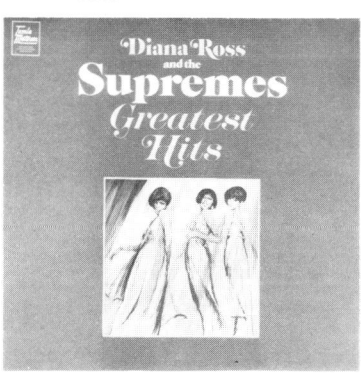

Diana Ross And The Supremes' Greatest Hits
Diana Ross & The Supremes

UK: Tamla Motown STML 11063
US: Motown 663
Produced by Holland-Dozier-Holland
Published 1972

Stop! In The Name Of Love
Nothing But Heartache
When The Lovelight Starts
 Shining Through His Eyes
My World Is Empty Without You
Where Did Our Love Go
Love Is Like An Itching In My
 Heart
Come See About Me
I Hear A Symphony
Reflections
Back In My Arms Again

63

You Keep Me Hanging On
Whisper You Love Me Boy
The Happening
Love Is Here & Now You're Gone
You Can't Hurry Love
Baby Love

Chosen number one by Clive James.

Even In The Quietest Moments
Supertramp

UK: AMLK 64634
US: A&M 4560
Produced by Supertramp
Published 1967

Give A Little Bit
Lover Boy
Even In The Quietest Moments

THE TOP 200 ALBUMS

King Crimson

Downstream
Babaji
From Now On
Fool's Overture

Chosen number one by Ritchie Yorke:
"To my ears this is rock's definitive statement about living in the super-70s. Supertramp are the worthy inheritors of rock's grand idealism as manifested in assorted music of the late 60s. Unlike most of their contemporaries, Supertramp obviously are not afraid to lash out at the complacency of the 70s, the era which pop writer Tom Wolfe has dubbed the 'Me' decade. For example, the superb tongue-in-cheek parody of contemporary life in 'From Now On'."

64

Mind Games
John Lennon

UK: PCS 7165
US: Cap. SW-3414
Produced by John Lennon
Published 1973

Mind Games
Tight As
Aisumasen (I'm Sorry)
One Day (At A Time)
Bring On The Lucy (Freda Peeple)
Nutopian International Anthem
Intuition
Out The Blue
Only People

I Know (I Know)
You Are Here
Meat City

Chosen number one by Loraine Alterman:
"Because the Beatles were the most earth-shaking group in rock and John is the most creative of them all and this is his most exciting, stimulating LP to date."

65

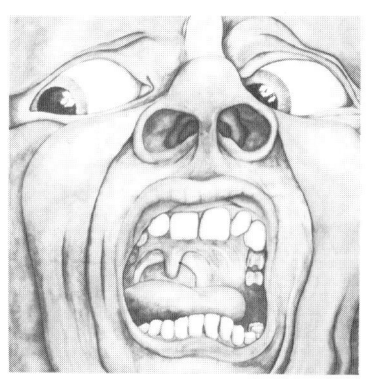

In The Court Of The Crimson King
King Crimson

UK: ILPS 9111
US: Atlantic 8245
Produced by King Crimson
Published 1969

21st Century Schizoid Man
I Talk To The Wind
Epitaph
Moonchild including The Dream and The Illusion
The Court Of The Crimson King including The Return Of The Fire Witch and The Dance Of The Puppets

66

Rock 'n' Roll
Elvis Presley

THE TOP 200 ALBUMS

UK: RCA Victor SF 8233
An English compilation album not released in America
Produced by various producers
Published 1972

Blue Suede Shoes
I Got A Sweetie (I Got A Woman)
I'm Counting On You
I'm Left, You're Right, She's Gone
That's All Right
Money Honey
Mystery Train
I'm Gonna Sit Right Down And Cry Over You
Trying To Get You
One-Sided Love Affair
Lawdy Miss Clawdy
Shake Rattle And Roll

Chosen number one by Ray Connolly.

67

Stand
Sly And The Family Stone

UK: Direction S8-63655
US: Epic 26456
Produced by Sly Stone
Published 1970

Stand
Don't Call Me Nigger Whitey
I Want To Take You Higher
Somebody's Watching You
Sing A Simple Song
Everyday People
Sex Machine
You Can Make It If You Try

Chosen number one by Don Topping 'El Numero Uno':

"A devastating performance by Sly & The Family Stone that had a profound influence on numerous other performers of the time."

68

Sticky Fingers
The Rolling Stones

UK: COC 59100
US: Rolling Stones 59100
Produced by Jimmy Miller
Published 1971

Brown Sugar
Sway
Wild Horses
Can't You Hear Me Knocking
You Gotta Move
Bitch
I Got The Blues
Sister Morphine
Dead Flowers
Moonlight Mile

Chosen number one by Herve Muller:
"The first one which came to my mind, so it's probably the right one. If it's rock we are talking about, it's got to be the Stones; if it's got to be an album as a whole, it's got to be **Sticky Fingers**. Just play it and you know why."

69

Sell Out
The Who

Sly Stone (Charles Gatewood)

UK: Track 612002
US: Decca 74950
Produced by Kit Lambert
Published 1967

Armenia City In The Sky
Heinz Baked Beans
Mary Anne With The Shaky Hand
Odorono
Tattoo
Our Love Was
I Can See For Miles
Can't Reach You
Medac
Relax
Silas Stingy
Sunrise
Rael

Love Me Tender
Anyway You Want Me
Too Much
Playing For Keeps
I'm All Shook Up
That's When Your Heartaches Begin
Loving You
Teddy Bear
Jailhouse Rock
Treat Me Nice
I Beg Of You
Don't
Wear My Ring Around Your Neck

Hard Headed Woman
I Got Stung
A Fool Such As I
A Big Hunk Of Love
Stuck On You
A Mess Of Blues
It's Now Or Never
I Gotta Know
Are You Lonesome Tonight?
Surrender
I Feel So Bad
Little Sister
Can't Help Falling In Love
Rock-A-Hula Baby
Anything That's Part Of You

Chosen number one by Ben Fong-Torres:
"Because it's imaginative, funny, and true to the spirit of rock and roll. In short, it has a good beat and you can laugh to it."

70

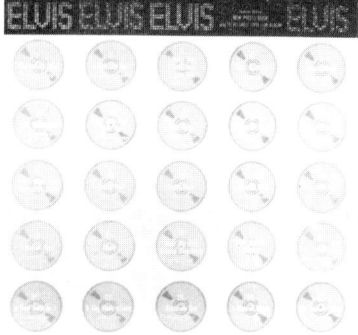

Worldwide 50 Gold Award Hits, Vol. 1
Elvis Presley

UK: RCA Victor LPM 6401
US: RCA Victor 6401
Produced by various producers
Published 1970

Heartbreak Hotel
I Was The One
I Want You, I Need You, I Love You
Don't Be Cruel
Hound Dog

Elvis Presley

THE TOP 200 ALBUMS

Good Luck Charm
She's Not You
Return To Sender
Where Do You Come From
One Broken Heart For Sale
(You're The) Devil In Disguise
Bossa Nova Baby
Kissin' Cousins
Viva Los Vegas
Ain't That Loving You Baby
Wooden Heart
Crying In The Chapel
If I Can Dream
In The Ghetto
Suspicious Minds
Don't Cry Daddy
Kentucky Rain
Elvis Sails

Chosen number one by Tim Rice:
"Greatest rock artist's greatest hits – and fifty of them in one 4 L.P. Album."

71

Back In The USA
MC5

UK: Atlantic K50346
US: Atlantic SD8247
Produced by Jon Landau
Published 1970

Tutti-Frutti
Tonight
Teenage Lust
Let Me Try
Looking At You
High School
Call Me Animal
The American Ruse
Shakin' Street

The Human Being Lawnmower
Back In The USA

72

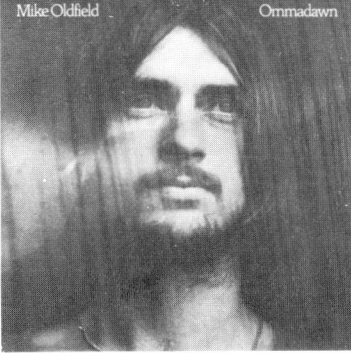

Ommadawn
Mike Oldfield

UK: Virgin Records V2043
US: PZ 33913
Produced by Mike Oldfield
Published 1975

Ommadawn Part I
Ommadawn Part II

73

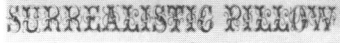

Surrealistic Pillow
Jefferson Airplane

UK: RCA SF 7889
US: RCA Victor 3766
Produced by Rick Jarrard
Published 1967

My Best Friend
3/5 Of A Mile In 10 Seconds
D.C.B.A.-25
How Do You Feel
Embryonic Journey
Don't Slip Away
Come Up The Years
Chauffeur Blues
Today
Comin' Back To Me
Somebody To Love

74

A Date With Elvis
Elvis Presley

UK: RCA RD27128
US: RCA Victor 2011
Produced by Elvis Presley
Published 1959

Blue Moon Of Kentucky
Milk Cow Blues Boogie
Baby Let's Play House
I Don't Care If The Sun Don't Shine
Tutti Frutti
I'm Gonna Sit Right Down And Cry
I Got A Woman
Good Rockin' Tonight
Is It So Strange
We're Gonna Move
Blue Moon
Just Because
One Sided Love Affair
Let Me

75

More Chuck Berry
Chuck Berry

UK: PYE NPL 28028
US: Chess 1465E
Compilation album
Published 1965

Sweet Little Rock & Roller
Anthony Boy
Little Queenie
Worried Life Blues
Carol
Reelin' & Rockin'
Thirty Days
Brown Eyed Handsome Man
Too Much Monkey Business
Wee Wee House
Jo Jo Gunne
Beautiful Delilah

76

Cheap Thrills
Big Brother & The Holding Company

UK: CBS 63392
US: Columbia 9700
Produced by John Simon
Published 1967

Combination Of The Two
I Need A Man To Love
Summertime
Piece Of My Heart
Turtle Blues
Oh, Sweet Mary
Ball And Chain

THE TOP 200 ALBUMS

77

Hard Nose The Highway
Van Morrison

UK: Warner Bros. K46242
US: War. 2712
Produced by Van Morrison
Published 1973

Snow In San Anselmo
Warm Love
Hard Nose The Highway

78

Wild Children
The Great Deception
Green
Autumn Song
Purple Heather

The Ronettes Sing Their Greatest Hits!
Ronettes featuring Veronica

UK: Phil Spector Int. Super 2307 003
US: PHL 4006
Produced by Phil Spector
Published 1964

Walking In The Rain
Do I Love You
So Young
(The Best Part Of) Breaking Up
I Wonder
What'd I Say
Be My Baby
You Baby
Baby, I Love You
How Does It Feel?
When I Saw You
Chapel Of Love

79

All Things Must Pass
George Harrison

UK: Apple STCH 639
US: Apple 639
Produced by George Harrison and Phil Spector
Published 1970

I'd Have You Anytime
My Sweet Lord
Wah-Wah
Isn't It A Pity (version one)
What Is Life
If Not For You
Behind That Locked Door
Let It Down
Run Of The Mill
Beware Of Darkness
Apple Scruffs
Ballad Of Sir Frankie Crisp (Let It Roll)
Awaiting On You All
All Things Must Pass

Van Morrison

THE TOP 200 ALBUMS

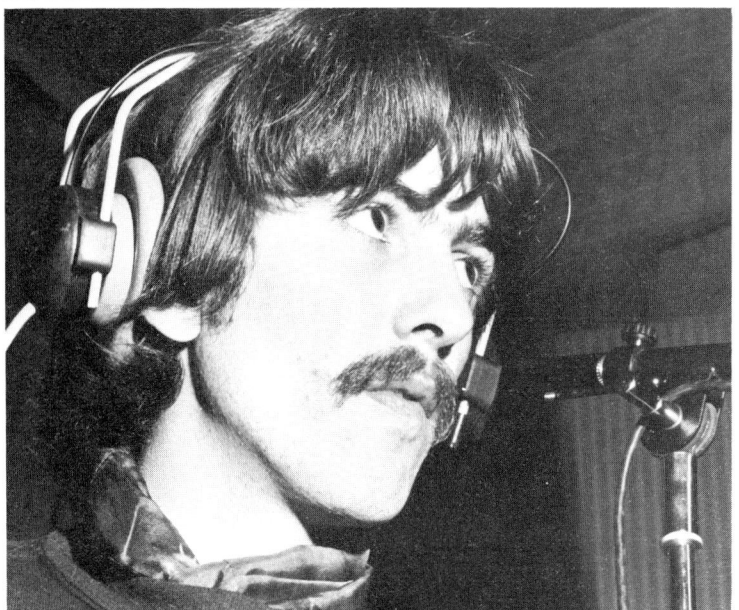

George Harrison (Leslie Bryce)

81

Lady Soul
Aretha Franklin

UK: Atlantic K 40016
US: Atlantic 8176
Produced by Jerry Wexler
Published 1972

Chain Of Fools
Money Won't Change You
People Get Ready
Niki Hoeky

I Dig Love
Art Of Dying
Isn't It A Pity (version two)
Hear Me Lord
Out Of The Blue
It's Johnny's Birthday
Plug Me In
I Remember Jeep
Thanks For The Pepperoni

Who Do You Love
Medley: Alabama Song,
  Backdoor Man, Love Hides,
  Five To One
Build Me A Woman
When The Music's Over
Close To You
Universal Wind
Break On Thru
The Celebration Of The Lizard
Soul Kitchen

80

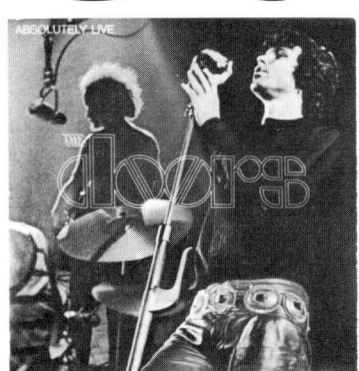

Absolutely Live
The Doors

UK: Elektra K62005
US: Elektra 2-9002
Produced by Paul A. Rothchild
Published 1976

Aretha Franklin

THE TOP 200 ALBUMS

UK: Decca LK 4852
US: London 499
Produced by Andrew Loog Oldham
Published 1967

Yesterday's Papers
My Obsession
Back Street Girl
Connection
She Smiled Sweetly
Cool, Calm & Collected
All Sold Out
Please Go Home
Who's Been Sleeping Here?
Complicated
Miss Amanda Jones
Something Happened To Me Yesterday

84

Buddy Holly's Greatest Hits
Buddy Holly

UK: MCA CDLM 8007
US: CRL 57492
Produced by Norman Petty
Published 1967

Peggy Sue
That'll Be The Day
Listen To Me
Everyday
Oh, Boy
Not Fade Away
Raining In My Heart
Maybe Baby
Rave On
Think It Over
It's So Easy
It Doesn't Matter Anymore
True Love Ways
Peggy Sue Got Married

(You Make Me Feel Like) A Natural Woman
Since You've Been Gone
Good To Me As I Am To You
Come Back Baby
Groovin'
Ain't No Way

Little Girl
Just A Little Bit
I Gave My Love A Diamond
Gloria
You Just Can't Win
Go On Home Baby
Don't Look Back
I Like It Like That
I'm Gonna Dress In Black
Bright Lights Big City
My Little Baby
(Get Your Kicks) On Route 66

82

The "Angry" Young Them
Them

Deleted
Produced by Tommy Scott
Published 1965

Mystic Eyes
If You And I Could Be As Two

83

Between The Buttons
The Rolling Stones

THE TOP 200 ALBUMS

85

Captain Fantastic And The Brown Dirt Cowboy
Elton John

UK: DJLPX 1
US: MCA 2142
Produced by Gus Dudgeon
Published 1975

Captain Fantastic And The
 Brown Dirt Cowboy
Tower Of Babel
Bitter Fingers
Tell Me When The Whistle Blows
Someone Saved My Life Tonight
(Gotta Get A) Meal Ticket
Better Off Dead
Writing
We All Fall In Love Sometimes
Curtains

86

Direct Hits
The Who

UK: Track 613 006
US: Not released in USA
Produced by Kit Lambert
Published 1969

Bucket "T"
I'm A Boy
Pictures Of Lily
Doctor! Doctor!
I Can See For Miles
Substitute
Happy Jack
The Last Time
In The City
Call Me Lightning
Mary Anne With The Shaky
 Hand
Dogs

87

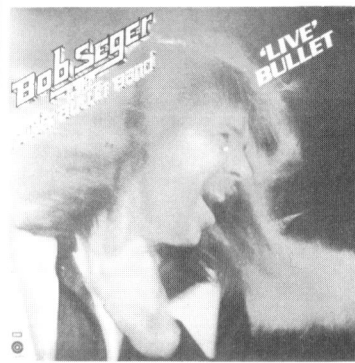

Live Bullet
Bob Seger & The Silver Bullet Band

UK: E-STSP 16
US: Capitol SKBB-11523
Produced by Bob Seger & Punch
Published 1976

Nutbush City Limits
Travellin' Man
Beautiful Loser
Jody Girl
I've Been Working
Turn The Page
U.M.C.
Bo Diddley
Ramblin' Gamblin' Man
Heavy Music
Katmandu
Lookin' Back
Get Out Of Denver
Let It Rock

Elton John

THE TOP 200 ALBUMS

Bob Seger

90

US: Bootleg AH-LP-3A

Tell Me Mama
I Don't Believe You
Baby Let Me Follow You Down
Just Like Tom Thumb Blues
Leopard Skin Pill-Box Hat
One Too Many Mornings
Ballad Of A Thin Man
Like A Rolling Stone

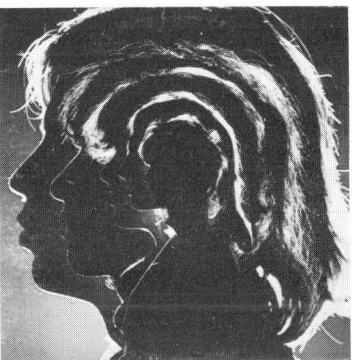

Hot Rocks 1964-1971
The Rolling Stones

UK: Compilation not released in England
US: London 606/7
Produced by Andrew Loog Oldham,
Jimmy Miller, The Rolling Stones
Published 1972

Time Is On My Side
Heart Of Stone
Play With Fire
(I Can't Get No) Satisfaction
As Tears Go By
Get Off My Cloud
Mother's Little Helper
19th Nervous Breakdown
Paint It Black
Under My Thumb
Ruby Tuesday
Let's Spend The Night Together
Jumping Jack Flash
Street Fighting Man
Sympathy For The Devil
Honky Tonk Women
Gimme Shelter
Midnight Rambler
You Can't Always Get What You
  Want
Brown Sugar
Wild Horses

88

Thank You
Heart Breaker
Livin' Lovin' Maid
(She's A Woman)
Ramble On
Moby Dick
Bring It On Home

89

In 1966 There Was . . .
Bob Dylan & The Band Live At
The Albert Hall

Led Zeppelin II
Led Zeppelin

UK: Atlantic K 40037
US: Atlantic 8236
Produced by Jimmy Page
Published 1971

Whole Lotta Love
What Is And What Should Never
  Be
The Lemon Song

THE TOP 200 ALBUMS

Stevie Wonder

93

You Are The Sunshine Of My Life
Maybe Your Baby
You And I
Tuesday Heartbreak
You've Got It Bad Girl
Superstition
Big Brother
Blame It On The Sun
Lookin' For Another Pure Love
I Believe (When I Fall In Love It Will Be Forever)

Electric Ladyland
Jimi Hendrix Experience

UK: Polydor 2657 012
US: Reprise 6307
Produced by Jimi Hendrix
Published 1968

And The Gods Made Love
Electric Ladyland
Crosstown Traffic
Voodoo Chile
Little Miss Strange
Long Hot Summer Night
Come On
Gipsy Eyes
Burning Of The Midnight Lamp
Rainy Day, Dream Away
1983 (A Merman I Should Turn To Be)
Moon, Turn The Tides... Gently Gently Away
Still Raining, Still Dreaming
House Burning Down
All Along The Watchtower
Voodoo Chile (slight return)

91

Night Owl Walk
Chinese Checkers
Home Grown
Mercy, Mercy
Plum-Nellie
Can't Be Still

Soul Dressing
Booker T & The MGs

Stax, deleted
Produced by Jim Stewart and Booker T & The MGs
Published 1972

Soul Dressing
Tic-Tac-Toe
Big Train
Jelly Bread
Aw' Mercy
Outrage

92

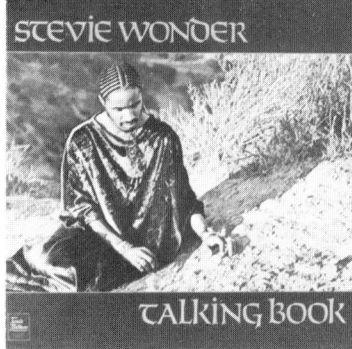

Talking Book
Stevie Wonder

UK: Tamla Motown STMA 8007
US: Tamla 319
Produced by Stevie Wonder
Published 1972

THE TOP 200 ALBUMS

94

Harvest
Neil Young

UK: Reprise K54005
US: Reprise 2032
Produced by Elliott Mazer & Neil Young
Published 1972

Out On The Weekend
Harvest
A Man Needs A Maid
Heart Of Gold
Are You Ready For The Country
Old Man
There's A World
Alabama
The Needle And The Damage Done
Words (Between The Lines Of Age)

95

12 Songs
Randy Newman

UK: K 44084
US: Reprise 6373
Produced by Lenny Waronker
Published 1969

Have You Seen My Baby?
Let's Burn Down The Cornfield
Mama Told Me Not To Come
Suzanne
Lover's Prayer
Lucinda
Underneath The Harlem Moon
Yellow Man
Old Kentucky Home
Rosemary
If You Need Oil
Uncle Bob's Midnight Blues

96

Cosmo's Factory
Creedence Clearwater Revival

UK: Fantasy FT 502
US: Fantasy 8402
Produced by John C Fogerty
Published 1970

Ramble Tamble
Before You Accuse Me
Travellin' Band
Ooby Dooby
Lookin' Out My Back Door
Run Through The Jungle
Up Around The Bend
My Baby Left Me
Who'll Stop The Rain
I Heard It Through The Grapevine
Long As I Can See The Light

Jimi Hendrix

THE TOP 200 ALBUMS

The Miracles (Rex Features)

99

Trashy Rumors
Slumming On Park Avenue
Biting My Nails
Danny
White Cadillac
American Man On The Moon
Girls

Chuck Berry's Golden Decade Vol. 2
Chuck Berry

UK: Chess 6641 058
US:
Album compiled by Nigel Grainge
Published 1973

Carol
You Never Can Tell
No Money Down
Together We Will Always Be
Mad Lad
Run Rudolph Run
Let It Rock
Sweet Little Rock And Roller
It Don't Take But A Few Minutes
I'm Talking About You
Driftin' Blues
Go Go Go
Jaguar And The Thunderbird
Little Queenie
Betty Jean
Guitar Boogie
Down The Road Apiece
Merry Christmas Baby
The Promised Land
Jo Jo Gunne
Don't You Lie To Me
Rockin' At The Philharmonic
La Juanda
Come On

97

My Baby Changes Like The Weather
Let Me Have Some
A Fork In The Road

98

Going To A Go-Go
Miracles

Deleted
Produced by Bill "Smokey" Robinson
Published 1965

The Tracks Of My Tears
Going To A Go-Go
Ooo Baby Baby
My Girl Has Gone
In Case You Need Love
Choosey Beggar
Since You Won My Heart
From Head To Toe
All That's Good

Romance Is On The Rise
Genevieve Waite

UK: Not released in England
US: Paramour PR 5088 SD
Produced by John Phillips
Published 1974

Loving Is Coming Back
Transient Friends
Times Of Love

Chuck Berry (Rex Features)

THE TOP 200 ALBUMS

100

The Buddy Holly Story
Buddy Holly

UK: Coral LVA 9105
US: Coral 57279
Produced by Norman Petty
Published 1959

Raining In My Heart
It Doesn't Matter Anymore
Early In The Morning
Maybe Baby
Peggy Sue
That'll Be The Day
Heartbeat
Everyday
Think It Over
Oh Boy
Rave On
It's So Easy

101

Bookends
Simon & Garfunkel

UK: CBS 63101
US: Columbia 9529
Produced by Paul Simon, Art Garfunkel & Roy Hales
Published 1967

Bookends
Save The Life Of My Child
America
Overs
Voices Of Old People
Old Friends
Bookends Theme
Fakin' It
Punky's Dilemma
Mrs Robinson
A Hazy Shade Of Winter
At The Zoo

102

Aretha's Gold
Aretha Franklin

UK: Atlantic K 40036
US: Atlantic 8227
Produced by Jerry Wexler
Published 1972

I Never Loved A Man (The Way I Love You)
Do Right Woman — Do Right Man
Respect
Dr. Feelgood
Baby, I Love You
(You Make Me Feel Like) A Natural Woman
Chain Of Fools
Since You've Been Gone (Sweet Sweet Baby)
Ain't No Way
Think
You Send Me
The House That Jack Built
I Say A Little Prayer
See Saw

103

Jackson Browne
Jackson Browne

UK: Asylum K 53022
US: Asylum 5051
Produced by Richard Sanford Orshoff
Published 1972

Jamaica Say You Will
A Child In These Hills
Song For Adam
Doctor My Eyes
From Silver Lake
Something Fine
Under The Falling Sky
Looking Into You
Rock Me On The Water
My Opening Farewell

104

Allman Brothers Band At Fillmore East
Allman Brothers Band

THE TOP 200 ALBUMS

Steve Miller

UK: Capricorn 2659 039
US: Capricorn 2802
Produced by Tom Dowd
Published 1971

Statesboro Blues
Done Somebody Wrong
They Call It Stormy Monday Blues
You Don't Love Me
Hot 'Lanta
In Memory Of Elizabeth Reed
Whipping Post

105

Sailor
The Steve Miller Band

UK: EMI ST 2984
US: Capitol 2984
Produced by The Steve Miller Band and Glyn Johns
Published 1968

Song For Our Ancestors
Dear Mary
My Friend
Living In The USA
Quicksilver Girl
Lucky Man
Gangster Of Love
You're So Fine
Overdrive
Dime-A-Dance Romance

106

What's Going On
Marvin Gaye

THE TOP 200 ALBUMS

UK: Tamla Motown STML 11190
US: Tamla 310
Produced by Marvin Gaye
Published 1971

What's Going On
What's Happening Brother
Flyin' High (In The Friendly Sky)
Save The Children
God Is Love
Mercy Mercy Me (The Ecology)
Right On
Wholy Holy
Inner City Blues (Make Me Wanna Holler)

107

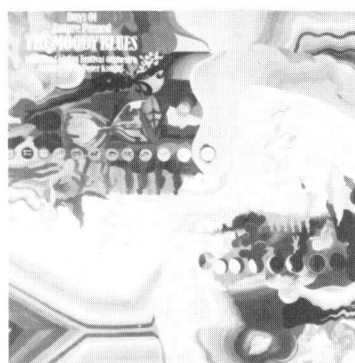

Days Of Future Passed
The Moody Blues

UK: Deram SML 707
US: Deram 1802
Executive producer Hugh Mendl
Published 1967

The Day Begins
Dawn: Dawn Is A Feeling
The Morning: Another Morning
Lunch Break: Peak Hour
The Afternoon: Forever Afternoon (Tuesday?)
The Afternoon: Time To Get Away
Evening: The Sun Set: Twilight Time
The Night: Nights In White Satin

108

Crime Of The Century
Supertramp

UK: A&M AMLS 68258
US: A&M 3647
Produced by Ken Scott and Supertramp
Published 1974

School
Bloody Well Right
Hide In Your Shell
Asylum
Dreamer
Rudy
If Everyone Was Listening
Crime Of The Century

109

Paradise And Lunch
Ry Cooder

UK: Reprise K 44260
US: Reprise 2179
Produced by Lenny Waronker and Russ Titelman
Published 1974

Tamp 'Em Up Solid
I'm A Fool For A Cigarette/Feelin' Good
Married Man's A Fool
Mexican Divorce
It's All Over Now
Tattler
Ditty Wa Ditty
If Walls Could Talk
Jesus On The Mainline

110

American Gothic
David Ackles

Ry Cooder (David Warner Ellis)

THE TOP 200 ALBUMS

UK: Elektra K42112
US: Elektra 75032
Produced by Bernie Taupin
Published 1972

American Gothic
Love's Enough
Ballad Of The Ship Of State
One Night Stand
Oh California
Another Friday Night
Family Band
Midnight Carousel
Waiting For The Moving Van
Blues For Billy Whitellond
Montana Song

111

Live At The Regal
B. B. King

UK: HMV CLP 1870
US: ABC 724
Live album
Published 1965

Everyday (I Have The Blues)
Sweet Little Angel
It's My Own Fault
How Blue Can You Get
Please Love Me
You Upset Me Baby
Worry, Worry
Woke Up This Morning
You Done Lost Your Good Thing Now
Help The Poor

112

Ramones
Ramones

UK: Sire BD 9103 253
US: Sire 7520
Produced by Craig Leon
Published 1976

Blitzkrieg Bop
Beat On The Brat
Judy Is A Punk
I Wanna Be Your Boyfriend
Chain Saw
Now I Wanna Sniff Some Glue
I Don't Wanna Go Down To The Basement
Loudmouth
Havana Affair
Listen To My Heart
53rd & 3rd
Let's Dance
I Don't Wanna Walk Around With You
Today Your Love, Tomorrow The World

113

Live At Carnegie Hall
Dory Previn

UK: United Artists UAD 60045/6
US: Artists LA 108-H
Produced by Nikolas Venet
Published 1973

Going Home
Mythical Kings And Iguanas
Scared To Be Alone
I Ain't His Child
I Dance And Dance And Smile and Smile
Esther's First Communion
The Veterans Big Parade
Play It Again, Sam
Michael Michael
Moon Rock
20 Mile Zone
Don't Put Him Down
Yada Yada La Scala
The Lady With The Braid
The Midget's Lament
Left Hand Lost
When A Man Wants A Woman
Angels And Devils The Following Day
Mary C Brown And The Hollywood Sign
Be Careful, Baby, Be Careful

114

Funhouse
The Stooges

UK: Elektra 42055
US: EKS 74071
Produced by Don Gallucci
Published 1970

Down On The Street
Loose
T.V. Eye
Dirt
1970
Funhouse
L.A. Blues

115

The Beach Boys' Greatest Hits
The Beach Boys

UK: Capitol ST 21628
US: (same as UK number)
Produced by James William Guercio
Published 1970

Sloop John B
California Girls
Barbara Ann
I Get Around
Wild Honey
I Can Hear Music
Darlin'
God Only Knows
Do It Again
Cottonfields
Bluebirds Over The Mountain
Then I Kissed Her
Help Me Rhonda
Break Away
Heroes And Villains
Good Vibrations

116

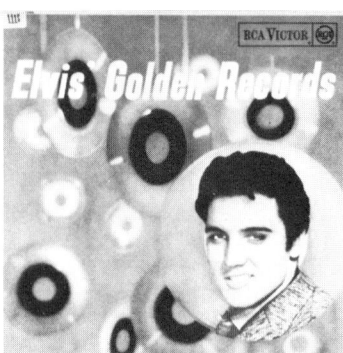

Elvis's Golden Records
Elvis Presley

UK: RCA RB 16069
US: RCA Victor 1707
Produced by Elvis Presley
Published 1958

Hound Dog
I Love You Because
All Shook Up
Heartbreak Hotel
Love Me
You're A Heartbreaker
Too Much
Don't Be Cruel
That's When Your Heartaches Begin
I'll Never Let You Go
Love Me Tender
I Forgot To Remember To Forget
Anyway You Want Me
I Want You, I Need You, I Love You

117

Nashville Skyline
Bob Dylan

UK: CBS 63601
US: Columbia 9825
Produced by Bob Johnston
Published 1969

Girl From The North Country
Nashville Skyline Rag
To Be Alone With You
I Threw It All Away
Peggy Day
Lay Lady Lay
One More Night
Tell Me That It Isn't True
Country Pie
Tonight I'll Be Staying Here With You

118

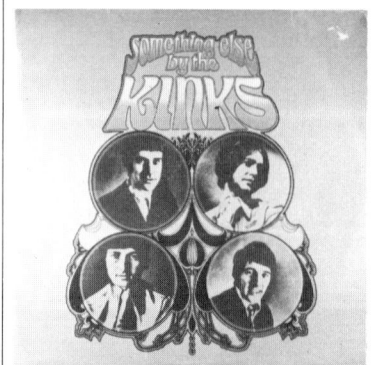

Something Else
The Kinks

THE TOP 200 ALBUMS

UK: Pye NPL 18193
US: Reprise 6279
Produced by Ray Davies
Published 1967

David Watts
Death Of A Clown
Two Sisters
No Return
Harry Ray
Tin Soldier Man
Situation Vacant
Love Me Till The Sun Shines
Lazy Old Sun
Afternoon Tea
Funny Face
End Of The Season
Waterloo Sunset

119

David Live
David Bowie At The Tower Philadelphia

UK: RCA APL2-0771
US: CPL 2-0772
Live Album
Published 1974

1984
Rebel Rebel
Moonage Daydream
Sweet Thing
Changes
Suffragette City
Aladdin Sane
All The Young Dudes
Cracked Actor
When You Rock'n'Roll With Me
Watch That Man
Knock On Wood
Diamond Dogs
Big Brother
Width Of A Circle
Jean Genie
Rock'n'Roll Suicide

120

Plastic Ono Band
John Lennon

UK: PCS 7124
USD: Apple 3372
Produced by John, Yoko and Phil Spector
Published 1970

Mother
Hold On John
I Found Out
Working Class Hero
Isolation
Remember
Love
Well Well Well
Look At Me
God
My Mummy's Dead

121

Led Zeppelin
Led Zeppelin

UK: Atlantic 40031
US: Atlantic 8216
Produced by Jimmy Page
Published 1968

Good Times Bad Times
Babe I'm Gonna Leave You
You Shook Me
Dazed And Confused
Your Time Is Gonna Come
Black Mountain Side
Communication Breakdown
I Can't Quit You Baby
How Many More Times

122

Goodbye Yellow Brick Road
Elton John

UK: DJLPD 1001
US: MCA 10003
Produced by Gus Dudgeon
Published 1973

Funeral For A Friend
Candle In The Wind
Bennie And The Jets
Goodbye Yellow Brick Road
Grey Seal
This Song Has No Title
Jamaica Jerk-Off
Sweet Painted Lady
I've Seen That Movie Too
The Ballad Of Danny Bailey (1909-34)
All The Girls Love Alice
Your Sister Can't Twist (But She Can Rock'n'Roll)
Saturday Night's Alright For Fighting
Roy Rogers
Social Disease
Harmony

THE TOP 200 ALBUMS

123

Axis: Bold As Love
Jimi Hendrix Experience

UK: Track 612003 2407 011
US: Reprise 6281
Produced by Chas. Chandler
Published 1968

Experience
Up From The Skies
Spanish Castle Magic
Wait Until Tomorrow
Ain't No Telling
Little Wing
If Six Was Nine
You've Got Me Floating
Castles Made Of Sand
She's So Fine

One Rainy Wish
Little Miss Lover
Bold As Love

124

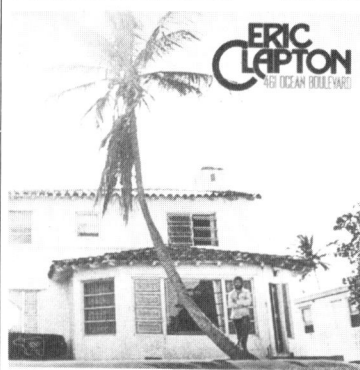

461 Ocean Boulevard
Eric Clapton

UK: RSO DeLuxe 2479 118
US: RSO 4801
Produced by Tom Dowd
Published 1974

Motherless Children
Give Me Strength
Willie And The Hand Jive
Get Ready
I Shot The Sheriff
I Can't Hold Out

Please Be With Me
Let It Grow
Steady Rollin' Man
Mainline Florida

125

White Light/White Heat
Velvet Underground

UK: 2353 024 Select
US: Verve 5046
Produced by Tom Wilson
Published 1967

White Light/White Heat
The Gift
Lady Godiva's Operation
Here She Comes Now
I Heard Her Call My Name
Sister Ray

126

Catch A Fire
The Wailers

THE TOP 200 ALBUMS

UK: ILPP 9241
US: Island 9241
Produced by Bob Marley and Chris Blackwell
Published 1973

Concrete Jungle
Slave Driver
400 Years
Stop That Train
Baby We've Got A Date (Rock It Baby)
Stir It Up
Kinky Reggae
No More Trouble
Midnight Ravers

127

Golden Archive Series
The Velvet Underground

US: MGM Gas 131
American compilation album not released in the UK
Published 1970

Candy Says
Sunday Morning
Femme Fatale
White Light White Heat
Jesus
Heroin
Beginning To See The Light
I'm Set Free
Here She Comes Now
Afterhours

Joe Cocker

128

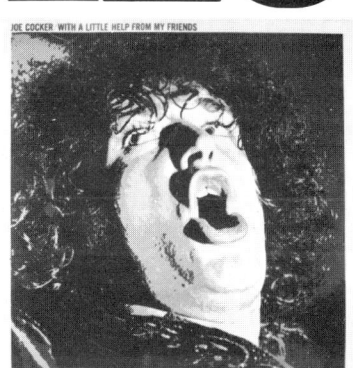

With A Little Help From My Friends
Joe Cocker

UK: MFP 5275
US: A&M 4182
Produced by Denny Cordell
Published 1968

Feeling Alright
Bye Bye Blackbird
Change In Louise
Marjorine
Just Like A Woman
Do I Still Figure In Your Life
Sandpaper Cadillac
Don't Let Me Be Misunderstood
With A Little Help From My Friends
I Shall Be Released

Bob Marley

THE TOP 200 ALBUMS

129

Wolfking Of L.A.
John Phillips

UK: EMI SSL 5027
US: Dunhill 50077
Produced by Lou Adler
Published 1970

April Anne
Down The Beach
Drum
Holland Tunnel
Let It Bleed, Genevieve
Malibu People
Mississippi
Someone's Sleeping
Captain
Topanga Canyon

130

John Prine
John Prine

UK: Atlantic K 40357
US: At. 8296
Produced by Arif Mardin
Published 1972

Illegal Smile
Spanish Pipedream
Hello In There
Sam Stone
Paradise
Pretty Good
Your Flag Decal Won't Get You Into Heaven Anymore
Far From Me
Angel From Montgomery
Quiet Man
Donald And Lydia
Six O'Clock News
Flashback Blues

131

Jonathan Richman And The Modern Lovers
Jonathan Richman And The Modern Lovers

UK: Beserkley BSERK 2
US: BZ 0048
Produced by Matthew King Kaufman and Glen Kolotkin
Published 1976

Rockin' Shopping Center
Back In The U.S.A.
Important In Your Life
New England
Lonely Financial Zone
Hi Dear
Abominable Snowman In The Market
Hey There Little Insect
Here Come The Martian Martians
Springtime
Amazing Grace

132

In Concert With The Edmonton Symphony Orchestra
Procul Harum

UK: Chrysalis CHR 1004
US: A&M 4335
Produced by Chris Thomas
Published 1971

Conquistador
Whaling Stories
A Salty Dog
All This And More
In Held 'Twas In I
Glimpses Of Nirvana
'Twas Teatime At The Circus
In The Autumn Of My Madness
I Know If I'd Been Wiser
Grand Finale

133

I Want To See The Bright Lights Tonight
Richard and Linda Thompson

THE TOP 200 ALBUMS

UK: Island ILPS-9266
US: Island ILPS-9266
Produced by Richard Thompson and John Wood
Published 1974

When I Get To The Border
Calvary Cross
Withered And Died
I Want To See The Bright Lights Tonight
Down Where The Drunkards Roll
We'll Sing Hallelujah
Has He Got A Friend For Me
The Little Beggar Girl
The End Of The Rainbow
The Great Valerio

134

Rockin' Pneumonia And The Boogie Woogie Flu
Huey 'Piano' Smith and The Clowns

UK: Deleted
US: Deleted
Produced by Johnny Vincent
Published 1965

Rockin' Pneumonia And The Boogie Woogie Flu Part I
Rockin' Pneumonia And The Boogie Woogie Flu Part II
Little Chicken Wah Wah
Little Liza Jane
Just A Lonely Clown
Hush Your Mouth
Don't You Know Yockomo
High Blood Pressure
Don't You Just Know It
Well I'll Be John Brown
Everybody's Whalin'
Havin' A Good Time
We Like Birdland
Talk To Me Baby

135

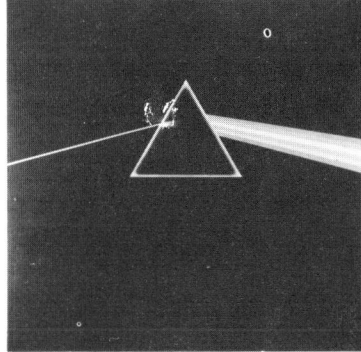

Dark Side Of The Moon
Pink Floyd

UK: EMI SHVL 804
US: Harv. SMAS-11163
Produced by Pink Floyd
Published 1973

Speak To Me
Breathe
On The Run
Time
The Great Gig In The Sky
Money
Us And Them
Any Colour You Like
Brain Damage
Eclipse

136

Johnny Burnette & His Rock'n'Roll Trio
Johnny Burnette

UK: Deleted
US: Deleted
Producer unknown
Published 1966

Honey Hush
Lonesome Train
Sweet Love On My Mind
Rock Billy Boogie
Lonesome Tears In My Eyes
All By Myself
The Train Kept A Rolling
I Just Found Out
Your Baby Blue Eyes
Chains Of Love
I Love You So
Drinking Wine, Spo-dee-o-dee, Drinking Wine

137

Motorvatin'
Chuck Berry

UK: Chess 9286 690
US: Not released US
Published 1977
Compilation Album

Johnny B Goode
Roll Over Beethoven
School Days
Maybellene
Rock And Roll Music
Oh Baby Doll
Too Much Monkey Business
Carol
Let It Rock
Sweet Little Rock and Roller
Bye Bye Johnny
Reelin' And Rockin'
No Particular Place To Go
Thirty Days
Sweet Little Sixteen
Little Queenie
Memphis
You Never Can Tell

THE TOP 200 ALBUMS

Diana Ross

Brown Eyed Handsome Man
Nadine
The Promised Land
Back In The USA

138

Magical Mystery Tour
The Beatles

UK: Parlophone PCTC 255
US: Capitol 2835
Produced by George Martin
Published 1967

Magical Mystery Tour
The Fool On The Hill
Flying
Blue Jay Way

Your Mother Should Know
I Am The Walrus
Hello Goodbye
Strawberry Fields Forever
Penny Lane
Baby You're A Rich Man
All You Need Is Love

139

John Wesley Harding
Bob Dylan

UK: CBS 63252
US: Columbia 9604
Produced by Bob Johnston
Published 1968

John Wesley Harding
As I Went Out One Morning
I Dreamed I Saw St. Augustine
All Along The Watchtower
The Ballad Of Frankie Lee And
    Judas Priest
Drifter's Escape
Dear Landlord
I Am A Lonesome Hobo
I Pity The Poor Immigrant
The Wicked Messenger
Down Along The Cove
I'll Be Your Baby Tonight

140

Motown Songbook — The Original Versions
Various Artists

UK: Tamla Motown STML 12026
Based on an American LP 'The Original Versions' but with different tracks.
A compilation LP
Produced by various producers
Published 1976

Where Did Our Love Go
Heat Wave
Please Mr Postman
Baby I Need Your Lovin'
How Sweet It Is (To Be Loved By
    You)
The Tracks Of My Tears
This Old Heart Of Mine (Is Weak
    For You)
Reach Out I'll Be There
Ain't Too Proud To Beg
You've Made Me So Very Happy
I Heard It Through The
    Grapevine
Take Me In Your Arms (Rock Me
    A Little While)
You're All I Need To Get By
Never Can Say Goodbye

THE TOP 200 ALBUMS

141

Their Greatest Hits 1971-1975
Eagles

UK: Asylum K 53017
US: Asylum 6E-105
Produced by Glyn Johns
Published 1976

Take It Easy
Witchy Woman
Lyin' Eyes
Already Gone
Desperado
One Of These Nights
Tequila Sunrise
Take It To The Limit
Peaceful Easy Feeling
Best Of My Love

142

For The Roses
Joni Mitchell

UK: Asylum K53007
US: Asylum 5057
Produced by Joni Mitchell
Published 1976

Banquet
Cold Blue Steel And Sweet Fire
Barngrill
Lesson In Survival
Let The Wind Carry Me
For The Roses
See You Sometime
Electricity
You Turn Me On I'm A Radio
Blonde In The Bleachers
Woman Of Heart And Mind
Judgement Of The Moon and
   Stars (Ludwig's Tune)

143

Crosby, Stills & Nash
David Crosby, Graham Nash &
Stephen Stills

The Eagles

THE TOP 200 ALBUMS

UK: Atlantic K40033
US: Atlantic 8229
Produced by Stephen Stills, David Crosby & Graham Nash
Published 1969

Suite: Judy Blue Eyes
Marrakesh Express
Guinnevere
You Don't Have To Cry
Pre-Road Downs
Wooden Ships
Lady Of The Island
Helplessly Hoping
Long Time Gone
49 Bye Byes

144

Joplin In Concert
Janis Joplin

UK: CBS 67241
US: Columbia 33160
Live Album
Published 1972

Down On Me
Bye, Bye Baby
All Is Loneliness
Piece Of My Heart
Road Block
Flower In The Sun
Summertime
Ego Rock
Half Moon
Kozmic Blues
Move Over
Try (Just A Little Bit Harder)
Get It While You Can
Ball And Chain

145

Joe Cocker
Joe Cocker

UK: Regal Zonophone SLRZ 1011
US: A&M 4224
Produced by Denny Cordell and Leon Russell
Published 1970

Dear Landlord
Bird On The Wire
Lawdy Miss Clawdy
She Came In Through The Bathroom Window
Hitchcock Railway
That's Your Business
Something
Delta Lady
Hello, Little Friend
Darling Be Home Soon

146

Wish You Were Here
Pink Floyd

UK: Harvest SHVL 814
US: Col. PC-33454
Produced by Pink Floyd
Published 1975

Shine On You Crazy Diamond (Part One)
Welcome To The Machine
Have A Cigar
Wish You Were Here
Shine On You Crazy Diamond (Part Two)

147

Live At Carnegie Hall
Chicago

UK: CBS S64508/9/10/11
US: GA-30863
Live Album
Published 1975

In The Country
Fancy Colours
Does Anybody Really Know What Time It Is
South California Purples
Question Sixty Seven & Sixty Eight
Sing A Meantune Kid
Beginnings
It Better End Soon
Introduction
Mother
Lowdown
Flight Six Hundred and Two
Motorboat To Mars
Free
Where Do We Go From Here
I Don't Want Your Money
Anxiety's Moment
West Virginia Fantasies
To Be Free
Happy 'Cause I'm Going Home

THE TOP 200 ALBUMS

Wake Up Sunshine (Ballet For A
   Girl In Buchanan)
Make Me Smile
So Much To Say, So Much To
   Give
Colour My World
No More Than Ever
A Song For Richard & His
   Friends
Twenty Five Or Six To Four
I'm A Man

148

Goodbye
Cream

UK: RSO 2394 178
US: Atco 7001
Produced by Felix Pappalardi
Published 1969

I'm So Glad
Politician
Sitting On Top Of The World
Badge
Doing That Scrapyard Thing
What A Bringdown

149

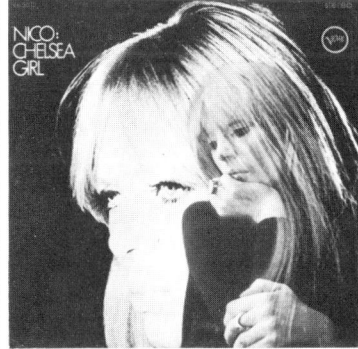

Chelsea Girl
Nico

UK: MGM Select 2353 025
US: MGS 1066
Produced by Tom Wilson
Published 1968

The Fairest Of The Seasons
These Days
Little Sister
Winter Song
It Was A Pleasure Then
Chelsea Girls
I'll Keep It With Mine
Somewhere There's A Feather
Wrap Your Troubles In Dreams
Eulogy To Lenny Bruce

150

Woodstock
Music From The Original
Soundtrack

UK: Atlantic K 60001
US: Cotillion 500
Produced by Eric Blackstead
Published 1970

I Had A Dream
Going Up The Country
Freedom
Rock & Soul Music
Coming Into Los Angeles
At The Hop
The "Fish" Cheer
I-Feel-Like-I'm-Fixin'-To-Die
   Rag
Drug Store Truck Drivin' Man
Joe Hill
Suite: Judy Blue Eyes
Sea Of Madness
Wooden Ships
We're Not Gonna Take It
With A Little Help From My
   Friends
Soul Sacrifice
I'm Going Home
Volunteers
Dance To The Music
Music Lover
I Want To Take You Higher
Rainbows All Over Your Blues
Love March
Star Spangled Banner
Purple Haze & Instrumental Solo

THE TOP 200 ALBUMS

151

Late For The Sky
Jackson Browne

UK: Asylum K43007
US: Asy 1017
Produced by Jackson Browne and
Al Schmitt
Published 1974

Late For The Sky
Fountain Of Sorrow
Farther On
The Late Show
The Road And The Sky
For A Dancer
Walking Slow
Before The Deluge

152

Blues Breakers
John Mayall & Eric Clapton

UK: Decca SKL 4804
US: London PS492
Produced by Mike Vernon
Published 1966

All Your Love
Hideaway
Little Girl
Another Man
Double Crossing Time
What'd I Say
Key To Love
Parchman Farm
Have You Heard
Ramblin' On My Mind
Steppin' Out
It Ain't Right

153

Presenting Dionne Warwick
Dionne Warwick

UK: Pye International NPL 28037, deleted
US: Deleted
Produced by Burt Bacharach
Published 1964

Make The Music Play
Anyone Who Had A Heart
Shall I Tell Her
Don't Make Me Over
I Cry Alone
Getting Ready For The
  Heartbreak
Oh Lord What Are You Doing To
  Me
Walk On By
Any Old Time Of Day
Mr. Heartbreak
Put Yourself In My Place
I Could Make You Mine
This Empty Place
Please Make Him Love Me

Jackson Browne (Jim Shea)

THE TOP 200 ALBUMS

154

The Notorious Byrd Brothers
The Byrds

UK: CBS 63169
US: Columbia 9575
Produced by Gary Usher
Published 1968

Artificial Energy
Goin' Back
Natural Harmony
Draft Morning
Wasn't Born To Follow
Get To You
Change Is Now
Old John Robertson
Tribal Gathering
Dolphins Smile
Space Odyssey

155

Paris 1919
John Cale

Jerry Garcia, Grateful Dead

UK: Island, deleted
US: Island, deleted
Produced by Chris Thomas
Published 1973

Child's Christmas In Wales
Hanky Panky Nohow
The Endless Plain Of Fortune
Andalucia
Macbeth
Paris 1919
Graham Greene
Half Past France
Antarctica Starts Here

156

American Beauty Rose
Grateful Dead

UK: Warner WS 1893
US: Warner Bros. 1893
Produced by the Grateful Dead
Published 1971

Box Of Rain
Friend Of The Devil
Sugar Magnolia
Operator
Candyman
Ripple
Brokedown Palace
Till The Morning Comes
Attics Of My Life
Truckin

157

Works Volume 1
Emerson Lake & Palmer

UK: Atlantic K80009
US: At. 7000
Produced by Greg Lake
Published 1977

Piano Concert No. 1
Lend Your Love To Me Tonight
C'est La Vie

THE TOP 200 ALBUMS

Emerson, Lake & Palmer

Hallowed Be Thy Name
Nobody Loves You Like I Do
Closer To Believing
The Enemy God
L.A. Nights
New Orleans
Bach Two Part Invention In D Minor
Food For Your Soul
Tank
Fanfare For The Common Man
Aaron Copland
Pirates

158

Hot Rats
Frank Zappa

UK: Reprise RSLP 6356
UK: Bizarre 6356
Produced by Frank Zappa
Published 1969

Peaches En Regalia
Willie The Pimp
Son Of Mr. Green Genes
Little Umbrellas
The Gumbo Variations
It Must Be A Camel

159

Playback
Appletree Theatre

UK: Verve 2353 051
US: Verve Forecast FTS 3042
Produced by John & Terrence Boylan
Published 1969

The Altogether Overture
...in the beginning...
Hightower Square (the start of it all)
Lullaby
Saturday Morning (about a Saturday morning)
Nevertheless It Was Italy (a deja vu in a pizza parlor, and a bit of merry olde England)
I Wonder If Louise Is Home (a bit of tragic relief)
Chez Louise
E-Train (the jello song)
Meanwhile
Brother Speed (vocal with didactic chorus)
You're The Biggest Thing In My Life (being, as it is, a pause in the proceeding)
Don't Blame It On Your Wife (the Fellini song: an ode or an elegy, depending on tomorrow)
The Sorry State Of Being Awake (an old banjo tune we rearranged)
Barefoot Boy (a bit of Johnny Appleseed)
Lotus Flower (Michael, John and Boona)
What A Way To Go (yes)

160

Dusty In Memphis
Dusty Springfield

Deleted
Produced by Jerry Wexler, Tom Dowd and Arif Mardin
Published 1968

Just A Little Lovin'
So Much Love
Son Of A Preacher Man
I Don't Want To Hear It Anymore
Don't Forget About Me
Breakfast In Bed
Just One Smile
The Windmills Of Your Mind
In The Land Of Make Believe
No Easy Way Down
I Can't Make It Alone

THE TOP 200 ALBUMS

161

Cigars, Acappella, Candy
The Belmonts

US: Buddah BDS 5123
Not released in the UK
Published 1972
Produced by Bob Feldman

That's My Desire
Da Doo Ron Ron
Loving You Is Sweeter Than Ever
Where Or When
My Sweet Lord
Rock And Roll Lullabye
We Belong Together

162

Na Na Hey Hey (Kiss Him Goodbye)
Street Corner Symphony

Electric Warrior
T. Rex

UK: Hifly 6
US: Reprise 6466
Produced by Tony Visconti
Published 1971

Mambo
Cosmic Dancer
Jeepster
Monolith
Lean Woman Blues
Get It On
Planet Queen
Girl
The Motivator
Life's A Gas
Rip Off

163

Beatles 1967-1970
The Beatles

UK: PCSP 718
US: Cap. SKBO 3404
Produced by George Martin
Published 1973

Strawberry Fields Forever
Penny Lane
Sgt. Pepper's Lonely Hearts Club Band
With A Little Help From My Friends
Lucy In The Sky With Diamonds
A Day In The Life
I Am The Walrus
Hello Goodbye
The Fool On The Hill
Magical Mystery Tour
Lady Madonna
Hey Jude
Back In The U.S.S.R.
While My Guitar Gently Weeps
Ob-La-Di, Ob-La-Da
Get Back
Don't Let Me Down
The Ballad Of John & Yoko
Old Brown Shoe
Here Comes The Sun
Come Together
Something
Octopus's Garden
Let It Be
Across The Universe
The Long And Winding Road

Marc Bolan

THE TOP 200 ALBUMS

164

Clouds
Joni Mitchell

UK: Reprise RSLP 6341
US: Reprise 6341
Produced by Paul Rothchild
Published 1969

Tin Angel
Chelsea Morning
I Don't Know Where I Stand
That Song About The Midway
Roses Blue
The Gallery
I Think I Understand
Songs To Aging Children Come
The Fiddle And The Drum
Both Sides, Now

165

The Rolling Stones No. 2
The Rolling Stones

UK: Decca LK 4661
US: London 402
Produced by Andrew Loog Oldham
Published 1964

Everybody Needs Somebody To Love
Down Home Girl
You Can't Catch Me
Time Is On My Side
What A Shame
Grown Up Wrong
Down The Road Apiece
Under The Boardwalk
I Can't Be Satisfied
Pain In My Heart
Off The Hook
Suzie-Q

166

Greatest Hits Vol. II
Smokey Robinson & The Miracles

US only compilation
US: Tam 5-280
Produced by Smokey Robinson
Published 1968

Going To A Go Go
My Girl Has Gone
More Love
000 Baby Baby
I Second That Emotion
Come On Do The Jerk
The Love I Saw In You Was Just A Mirage
The Tracks Of My Tears
(Come 'Round Here) I'm The One You Need
Whole Lot Of Shakin' In My Head (Since I Met You)
Choosy Beggar
Save Me

THE TOP 200 ALBUMS

167

Otis Redding In Europe
Otis Redding

UK: ATCO 228 017
US: ATCO 33-286
Live Album
Published 1968

Respect
I Can't Turn You Loose
I've Been Loving You Too Long
My Girl
Shake
(I Can't Get No) Satisfaction
Fa Fa Fa Fa Fa (Sad Song)
These Arms Of Mine
Day Tripper
Try A Little Tenderness

168

Bridge Over Troubled Water
Simon and Garfunkel

UK: CBS 63699
US: Columbia 9914
Produced by Paul Simon, Arthur Garfunkel, Roy Halee
Published 1970

Bridge Over Troubled Water
El Condor Pasa
Cecilia
Keep The Customer Satisfied
So Long, Frank Lloyd Wright
The Boxer
Baby Driver
The Only Living Boy In New York
Why Don't You Write Me
Bye Bye Love
Song For The Asking

169

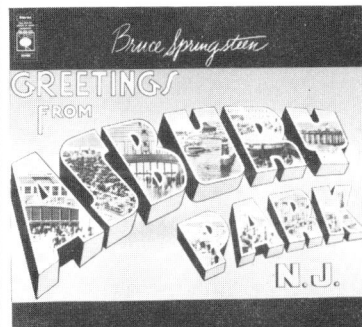

Greetings From Asbury Park N.J.
Bruce Springsteen

UK: CBS 65480
US: Col. PC-31903
Produced by Mike Appel and Jim Cretecos
Published 1973

Blinded By The Light
Growin' Up
Mary Queen Of Arkansas
Does This Bus Stop At 82nd Street?
Lost In The Flood
The Angel
For You
Spirit In The Night
It's Hard To Be A Saint In The City

170

Hunky Dory
David Bowie

UK: RCA SF 8244
US: RCA Victor 4623
Produced by Ken Scott
Published 1971

Changes
Oh! You Pretty Things
Eight Line Poem

THE TOP 200 ALBUMS

Life On Mars
Kooks
Quicksand
Fill Your Heart
Andy Warhol
Song For Bob Dylan
Queen Bitch
The Bewlay Brother

171

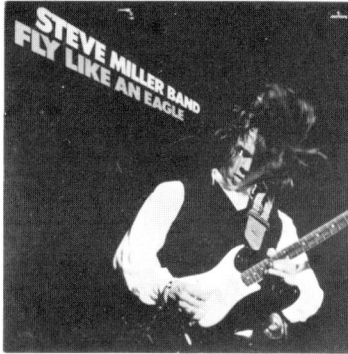

Fly Like An Eagle
Steve Miller Band

UK: Mercury 9286 177
US: Cap. ST-11497
Produced by Steve Miller
Published 1976

Fly Like An Eagle
Space Odyssey
Wild Mountain Honey
Serenade
Dance, Dance, Dance
Mercury Blues
Take The Money And Run
Rock'n Me
You Send Me
Blue Odyssey
Sweet Maree
The Window

172

A Man And His Soul
Ray Charles

US: ABCS 590X
Not released in the UK
Published 1967

I Can't Stop Loving You
What'd I Say
Old Man River
One Mint Julep
Crying Time
Makin' Whoopee
Busted
Takes Two To Tango
Ruby
Let's Go Get Stoned
Cry
Unchain My Heart
Georgia On My Mind
Baby It's Cold Outside
Worried Mind
I Chose To Sing The Blues
I Don't Need No Doctor
Born To Lose
Hit The Road Jack
You Are My Sunshine
From The Heart
Teardrops From My Eyes
No Use Crying
Chitlins With Candied Yams

173

Rock 'N' Roll Animal
Lou Reed

UK: RCA APL 1-0472
US: RCA APL 1-0472
Produced by Steve Katz and Lou Reed
Published 1966

Intro
Sweet Jane
Heroin
White Light White Heat
Lady Day
Rock'n'Roll

Ray Charles (Annie Leibovitz)

THE TOP 200 ALBUMS

Traffic

176

The Low Spark Of High Heeled Boys
Traffic

UK: Island ILPS 9180
US: Island 9306
Produced by Steve Winwood
Published 1971

Hidden Treasure
The Low Spark Of High-Heeled
   Boys
Rock'n'Roll Stew
Many A Mile To Freedom
Light Up Or Leave Me Alone
Rainmaker

174

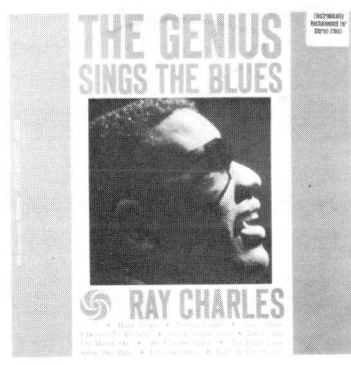

Genius Sings The Blues
Ray Charles

UK: London LT 2-K15238
US: Atlantic 8052
Producer unknown
Published 1960

Early In The Morning
Hard Times (No One Knows
   Better Than I)
The Midnight Hour
The Right Time
Feelin' Sad
Ray's Blues
I'm Moving On
I Believe To My Soul
Nobody Cares
Mr. Charles' Blues

175

Some Day Baby
I Wonder Who

Shoot Out At The Fantasy Factory
Traffic

UK: Island ILPS 9224
US: Is. 9224
Produced by Steve Winwood and
Jim Capaldi
Published 1973

Shoot Out At The Fantasy
   Factory
Roll Right Stones
Evening Blue
Tragic Magic
(Sometimes I Feel So)
   "Uninspired"

177

The Soft Machine
The Soft Machine

UK: Probe CPLP 4500
US: Probe 4500

THE TOP 200 ALBUMS

Produced by Chas Chandler and Tom Wilson
Published 1969

Hope For Happiness
Joy Of A Toy
Hope For Happiness (reprise)
Why Am I So Short?
So Boot If At All
A Certain Kind
Save Yourself
Priscilla
Lullabye Letter
We Did It Again
Plus Belle Qu'une Poubelle
Why Are We Sleeping?
Box 25/4 Lid

178

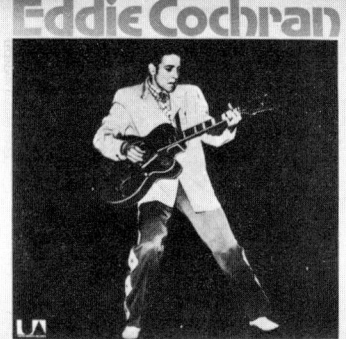

Legendary Masters
Eddie Cochran

UK: United Artists UAD 60017/8
US: Artists 9959
A compilation album produced by various people
Published 1972

Skinny Jim
Let's Get Together
Eddie's Blues
Little Lou
Pink Pegged Slacks
Jeanie Jeanie Jeanie
Something Else
Pretty Little Devil
Who Can I Count On
Thinkin' About You
Opportunity
Latch On
I'm Ready
Three Stars
Cotton Picker
Summertime Blues
Cut Across Shorty
Milk Cow Blues
My Way
Blue Suede Shoes
Nervous Breakdown
Come On Everybody
Sittin' In The Balcony
Twenty Flight Rock
Teenage Cutie
Hallelujah, I Love Her So
Fourth Man Theme
Weekend
Bo Weevil
Long Tall Sally

Eddie Cochran

THE TOP 200 ALBUMS

179

Grievous Angel
Gram Parsons with Emmylou Harris

UK: Reprise K 54018
US: Reprise 2171
Produced by Gram Parsons
Published 1974

Return Of The Grievous Angel
Hearts On Fire
I Can't Dance
Brass Buttons
$1000 Wedding
Cash On The Barrelhead
Hickory Wind
Love Hurts
Las Vegas
In My Hour Of Darkness

180

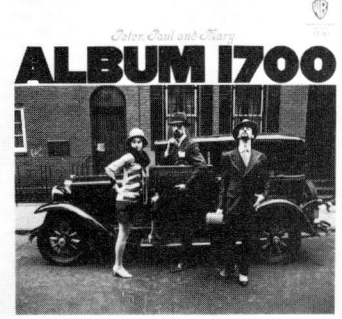

Album 1700
Peter, Paul and Mary

UK: Warner Brothers, deleted
US: Warner Brothers, deleted
Produced by Al Grossman and Milton Okun
Published mid 60s

Rolling Home
Leaving On A Jet Plane
Weep For Jamie
No Other Name
The House Song
The Great Mandella (The Wheel Of Life)
I Dig Rock And Roll Music
If I Had Wings
I'm In Love With A Big Blue Frog
Whatshername
Bob Dylan's Dream
The Song Is Love

181

King Of The Delta Blues Singers
Robert Johnson

UK: CBS M64102
US: Col. CL-1654
Produced by Frank Driggs
Published 1970

Kind Hearted Woman Blues
I Believe I'll Dust My Broom
Sweet Home Chicago
Rambling On My Mind
Phonograph Blues
They're Red Hot
Dead Shrimp Blues
Preachin' Blues
I'm A Steady Rollin' Man
From Four Till Late
Little Queen Of Spades
Malted Milk
Drunken Hearted Man
Stop Breakin' Down Blues
Honeymoon Blues
Love In Vain

182

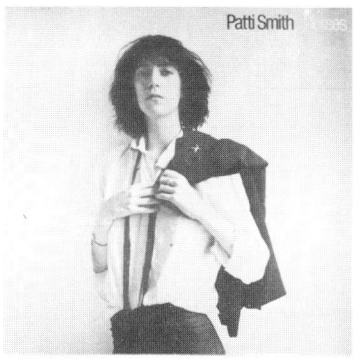

Horses
Patti Smith

UK: Arista Arty 122
US: Ari. 4066
Produced by John Cale
Published 1975

Gloria
Redondo Beach
Birdland
Free Money
Kimberly
Break It Up
Land
Elegie

183

Mendocino
Sir Douglas Quintet

UK: Oval OVLM 5001
US: Smash 67115
Produced by Doug Sahm
Published 1975

THE TOP 200 ALBUMS

Holger Czukay, Can

184

Ege Bamyasi
Can

UK: UAS 29414
US: U. Artists LA 063G
Produced by Can
Published 1972

Mendocino
I Don't Want
I Wanna Be Your Mama Again
At The Crossroads
If You Really Want Me To, I'll Go
And It Didn't Even Bring Me Down
Lawd, I'm Just A Country Boy In This Great Big Freaky City
She's About A Mover
Texas Me
Oh Baby, It Just Don't Matter

Pinch
Sing Swan Song
One More Night
Vitamin C
Soup
I'm So Green
Spoon

185

Holland
The Beach Boys

UK: Reprise K 54008
US: War. 2118
Produced by The Beach Boys
Published 1972

Sail On Sailor
Steam Boat
California Saga/Big Sur
California Saga/The Beaks Of Eagles
California Saga/California
The Trader
Leaving This Town
Only With You
Funky Pretty

186

Chuck Berry's Golden Decade
Chuck Berry

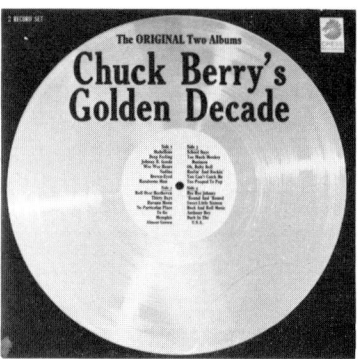

UK: Chess 6499 084/5
US: Chess 1514
Compilation album
Published 1972

Maybellene
Deep Feeling
Johnny B. Goode
Wee Wee Hours
Nadine
Brown-Eyed Handsome Man
Roll Over Beethoven
Thirty Days
Havana Moon
No Particular Place To Go
Memphis
Almost Grown
School Days
Too Much Monkey Business
Oh, Baby Doll
Reelin' And Rockin'
You Can't Catch Me
Too Pooped To Pop
Bye Bye Johnny
'Round And 'Round
Sweet Little Sixteen
Rock And Roll Music
Anthony Boy
Back In The U.S.A.

THE TOP 200 ALBUMS

187

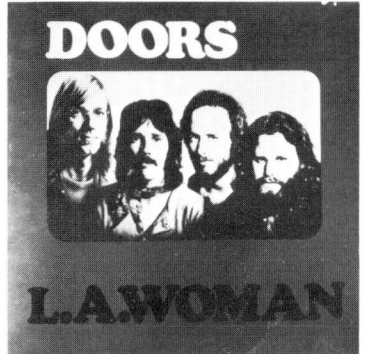

L.A. Woman
The Doors

UK: Elektra EKS 75011
US: Elektra 75011
Produced by Bruce Botnick and The Doors
Published 1976

The Changeling
Love Her Madly
Been Down So Long
Cars Hiss By My Window
L.A. Woman
L'America
Hyacinth House
Crawling King Snake
The WASP (Texas Radio And
　The Big Beat)
Riders On The Storm

188

UK: Columbia 335X1512
US: Not released USA
Produced by Norrie Paramor
Published 1963

Move It!
Living Doll
Travelin' Light
A Voice In The Wilderness
Fall In Love With You
Please Don't Tease
Nine Times Out Of Ten
I Love You
Theme For A Dream
A Girl Like You
When The Girl In Your Arms Is
　The Girl In Your Heart
The Young Ones
I'm Looking Out The Window
Do You Want To Dance

189

Live At Monterey
Otis Redding/The Jimi Hendrix Experience

UK: Deleted
US: Reprise 2029
Produced by Lou Adler and John Phillips
Published 1970

Like A Rolling Stone
Rock Me, Baby
Can You See Me
Wild Thing
Shake
Respect
I've Been Loving You Too Long
(I Can't Get No) Satisfaction
Try A Little Tenderness

190

One Of These Nights
The Eagles

UK: Asylum K 53014
US: Asy 1039
Produced by Bill Szymczyk
Published 1976

One Of These Nights
Too Many Hands

Cliff Richard & The Shadows (Rex Features)

THE TOP 200 ALBUMS

Chicago

UK: Swan Song SSK 89400
US: Swan 200
Produced by Jimmy Page
Published 1975

Custard Pie
The Rover
In My Time Of Dying
Houses Of The Holy
Trampled Under Foot
Kashmir
In The Light
Bron-Yr-Aur
Down By The Seaside
Ten Years Gone
Night Flight
The Wanton Song
Boogie With Stu
Black Country Woman
Sick Again

193

Chicago IX — Chicago's Greatest Hits
Chicago

UK: CBS 69222
US: Col. PC-33900
Produced by James William Guercio
Published 1975

25 Or 6 To 4
Does Anybody Really Know What Time It Is?
Colour My World
Just You 'n' Me
Saturday In The Park
Never Been In Love Before
Feelin' Stronger Every Day
I'm A Man
Make Me Smile
Wishing You Were Here
Call On Me
(I've Been) Searchin' So Long
Beginnings

Hollywood Waltz
Journey Of The Sorcerer
Lyin' Eyes
Take It To The Limit
Visions
After The Thrill Is Gone
I Wish You Peace

Candy Says
What Goes On
Some Kinda Love
Pale Blue Eyes
Jesus
Beginning To See The Light
I'm Set Free
That's The Story Of My life
The Murder Mystery
Afterhours

191

The Velvet Underground
Velvet Underground

UK: MGM Select 2353 022
US: MGM 4617
Produced by Val Valentine
Published 1969

192

Physical Graffiti
Led Zeppelin

Robert Plant, Led Zeppelin

THE TOP 200 ALBUMS

194

Taking Tiger Mountain
Eno

UK: Island ILPS 9309
US: Is 9309
Produced by Eno
Published 1974

Burning Airlines Give You So
 Much More
Back In Judy's Jungle
The Fat Lady Of Limbourg
Mother Whale Eyeless
The Great Pretender
Third Uncle
Put A Straw Under Baby
The True Wheel
China My China
Taking Tiger Mountain

195

Solid Gold Soul
Various Artists

UK: Deleted
US: Atlantic 8116
Compilation Album
Published 1966

Got To Get You Off My Mind
Don't Fight It
I Want To (Do Everything For
 You)
See-Saw
Don't Play That Song
Mr. Pitiful
In The Midnight Hour
Hold What You've Got
Mercy, Mercy
I've Been Loving You Too Long
Just Out Of Reach
Stand By Me

196

Sound Of '65
Graham Bond

UK: Deleted
US: Deleted
Produced by Robert Stigwood
Published 1965

Hoochie Coochie
Baby Make Love To Me
Neighbour Neighbour
Early In The Morning
Spanish Blues
Oh Baby
Little Girl
I Want You
Wade In The Water
Got My Mojo Working
Train Time
Baby Be Good To Me
Half A Man
Tammy

197

Everything is Everything
Donny Hathaway

UK: Atco Standard 2465 019
US: Atco 332
Produced by Donny Hathaway and Ric
Powell
Published 1971

Voices Inside (Everything Is
 Everything)
Je Vous Aime (I Love You)
I Believe To My Soul
Misty
Sugar Lee
Tryin' Times
Thank You Master (For My Soul)
The Ghetto
To Be Young, Gifted And Black

198

The Temptations' Greatest Hits
The Temptations

THE TOP 200 ALBUMS

UK: STML 11042
US: Gordy 919
Produced by Smokey Robinson, Ronald White, Norman Whitfield
Published 1966

The Way You Do The Things You Do
My Girl
Ain't Too Proud To Beg
Don't Look Back
Get Ready
Beauty Is Only Skin Deep
Since I Lost My Baby
The Girl's Alright With Me
My Baby
It's Growing
I'll Be In Trouble
Girl (Why You Wanna' Make Me Blue)

199

New York Dolls
New York Dolls

UK: Mercury 6338 270
US: Mercury SRM 1-675
Produced by Todd Rundgren
Published 1973

Personality Crisis
Looking For A Kiss
Vietnamese Baby
Lonely Planet Boy
Frankenstein
Trash
Bad Girl
Subway Train
Pills
Private World
Jet Boy

200

Mixed Bag
Richie Havens

UK: Verve Select 2317 002
US: Verve Forecast 3006
Produced by Jerry Schoenbaum
Published 1967

High Flyin' Bird
I Can't Make It Anymore
Morning, Morning
Adam
Follow
Three Day Eternity
Sandy
Handsome Johnny
San Francisco Bay Blues
Just Like A Woman
Eleanor Rigby

The Rock Critics and DJ's

The contributors and their personal Top 10 album selections.

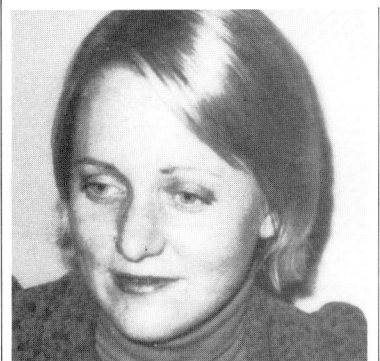

Loraine Alterman

A New York freelance writer, Loraine has spent stints running the local office of *Rolling Stone* and contributing regularly to the *New York Sunday Times*.

1. **Mind Games** (64)
   John Lennon
2. **There Goes Rhymin' Simon** (44)
   Paul Simon
3. **Live at Carnegie Hall** (113)
   Dory Previn
4. **The Beatles 1962-1966** (38)
   The Beatles 1967-1970 (163)
   Beatles
5. **The Immortal Otis Redding** (33)
   Otis Redding
6. **A Man and His Soul** (172)
   Ray Charles
7. **The Harder They Come** (26)
   Soundtrack From the Film
8. **Lady Soul** (81)
   Aretha Franklin
9. **For the Roses** (142)
   Joni Mitchell
10. **Sail Away**
    Randy Newman

Leonard J Beer

As Vice-President, Marketing for *Record World*, Lenny Beer supervised the chart department of the magazine when it won its reputation for unusual accuracy and integrity.

1. **Born to Run** (10)
   Bruce Springsteen
2. **Sergeant Pepper's Lonely Hearts Club Band** (1)
   Beatles
3. **Layla And Other Assorted Love Songs** (15)
   Derek and the Dominoes
4. **John Prine** (130)
   John Prine
5. **Plastic Ono Band** (120)
   John Lennon
6. **Blonde on Blonde** (2)
   Bob Dylan
7. **Tapestry** (21)
   Carole King
8. **The Rise and Fall of Ziggy Stardust** (47)
   David Bowie
9. **Ladies of the Canyon**
   Joni Mitchell
10. **Jesse Winchester**
    Jesse Winchester

Chuck Blore

One of the great innovators in pop radio history, Chuck Blore now runs a syndication service in Hollywood.

1. **Average White Band** (59)
   Average White Band
2. **Let It Bleed** (8)
   Rolling Stones
3. **Allman Brothers Band At Filmore East** (104)
   Allman Brothers Band
4. **David Live** (119)
   David Bowie
5. **Led Zeppelin IV** (29)
   Led Zeppelin
6. **Low Spark of High-Heeled Boys** (176)
   Traffic
7. **Every Picture Tells a Story** (46)
   Rod Stewart
8. **Hotel California**
   Eagles
9. **Cheap Thrills** (76)
   Big Brother and the Holding Company
10. **Surrealistic Pillow** (73)
    Jefferson Airplane

Geoffrey Cannon

Weekly rock commentator in the Guardian between 1968 and 1972. He was also involved with the British Granada Television team in 1968/69 when they made three documentaries, 'Stones In The

THE ROCK CRITICS & DJ'S

Park', 'The Doors Are Open' and 'Johnny Cash At San Quentin'. Now editor of the "Radio Times".

1. **Blood on the Tracks** (25) — Bob Dylan
2. **The "Angry" Young Them** (82) — Them
3. **Born to Run** (10) — Bruce Springsteen
4. **The Velvet Underground and Nico** (14)
5. **Forever Changes** (16) — Love
6. **The Rolling Stones No. 2** (165) — Rolling Stones
7. **L.A. Woman** (187) — Doors
8. **Summer Days** — Beach Boys
9. **Tommy** (32) — Who
10. **Sunny Afternoon** — Kinks / **Beat and Soul** — Everly Brothers

Roy Carr

The author of *The Beatles: An Illustrated Record* and *The Rolling Stones: An Illustrated Record*, Roy Carr of the *New Musical Express* has completed work on a 64-part radio series for North American syndication.

1. **Blonde on Blonde** (2) — Bob Dylan
2. **Revolver** (6) — Beatles
3. **Motorvatin'** (137) — Chuck Berry
4. **Are You Experienced?** (17) — Jimi Hendrix Experience
5. **Back in the USA** (71) — MC5
6. **The Sun Collection** (11) — Elvis Presley
7. **Exile on Main Street** (7) — Rolling Stones
8. **Leave Home** — Ramones
9. **The Velvet Underground and Nico** (14)
10. **Meaty, Beaty, Big and Bouncy** (55) — Who

"Mission Impossible: attempting to select just ten albums and cover all bases is like trying to write the aesthetics of rock on the head of a pin. Though there were many instances when 'Best Of' compilations offer a far more accurate insight into an artist's work, I have restricted my choice to cover just Chuck Berry and The Who.

"I have based my personal selection on those albums which either revolutionised or, at critical junctures, re-affirmed the true ethos and sheer excitement that can only be found in rock 'n' roll music."

John Collis

The Music Editor of *Time Out*, John Collis' duties include compiling The Other Singles Chart, which bears relation to no other.

1. **The Chirping Crickets** (60) — Buddy Holly and the Crickets
2. **Buddy Holly's Greatest Hits** (84) — Buddy Holly
3. **Chuck Berry's Golden Decade Vol. 2** (99) — Chuck Berry
4. **Nashville Skyline** (117) — Bob Dylan
5. **Elvis Golden Records Vol. 1** (116) — Elvis Presley
6. **Legendary Masters** (178) — Eddie Cochran
7. **All Them Blues** — Elmore James
8. **The Original** — Carl Perkins
9. **Dreaming My Dreams** — Waylon Jennings
10. **The Best of Stan Freberg** — Stan Freberg

"None of the above are unusual, but it was agonising to leave out David Ackles, Fogerty/Creedence, the Coasters, Noel Coward, the Everlys, Haggard, Cash, Spike Jones, Jerry Lee, Parton, Doug Sahm, Jack Scott, the Shangri-Las and New Orleans R&B. My insistence on living in the past explains the number of compilation albums – the best albums are usually a collection of singles anyway."

Ray Connolly

Screen writer of 'Stardust' and 'That'll Be the Day', Ray is also known as an author, playwright and journalist.

THE ROCK CRITICS & DJ'S

1	**Rock 'n' Roll** (66)	Elvis Presley
2	**Harvest** (94)	Neil Young
3	**Bookends** (101)	Simon and Garfunkel
4	**Imagine** (28)	John Lennon
5	**Presenting Dionne Warwick** (153)	Dionne Warwick
6	**Clouds** (164)	Joni Mitchell
7	**After the Goldrush** (40)	Neil Young
8	**Elton John's Greatest Hits** (US version)	Elton John
9	**Love Songs**	Beatles
10	**Tim Hardin 1**	Tim Hardin

"I have chosen two compilation albums and several which included hit singles on them because basically I'm a fan of singles much more than albums. Indeed, although I buy albums all the time I generally tape three or four selections from them and then put the album away and only play my favourite tracks."

Jonathan Cott

The Renaissance Man of rock criticism, Jonathan Cott has absorbed so much he is the only journalist in the field capable of writing: "'Sunny Afternoon', 'Waterloo Sunset', or 'Sitting by the Riverside' suggest the world of T'ang Chinese poets conversing and drinking wine by moonlight, or, closer to home, the streams and meadows of Izaak Walton's angler".

1	**Rubber Soul** (5)	Beatles
2	**Bringing It All Back Home** (27)	Bob Dylan
3	**The Band** (13)	The Band
4	**Astral Weeks** (4)	Van Morrison
5	**Exile on Main Street** (7)	Rolling Stones
6	**Greatest Hits, Vol. 2** (166)	Smokey Robinson and the Miracles
7	**The Immortal Otis Redding** (33)	Otis Redding
8	**Pet Sounds** (12)	Beach Boys
9	**The Village Green Preservation Society**	Kinks
10	**Plastic Ono Band** (120)	John Lennon

"'Rock' — as well as rock and roll — is nothing without its blues, gospel, R&B, bluegrass, and country antecedents. And any list of the best rock albums that neglected to mention its debt specifically to Tampa Red, Washboard Sam, the Harlem Hamfats, Professor Longhair, Arthur Crudup, Elmore James, Howlin' Wolf, The Rev. R. H. Harris, The Swan Silverstones, Marion Williams, Charlie Poole, the Monroe Brothers, the Stanley Brothers, et al. would be jejune and provincial. Any list that forgot about rock and roll auteurs like Chuck Berry, Buddy Holly, Elvis, Little Richard, and Eddie Cochran would be equally dismal. Any list that did not regret the omission of singles classics like 'Maybe', 'Give Him A Great Big Kiss', 'Itchycoo Park', 'Road Runner', 'I Can't Explain', or 'Up Around the Bend' would reflect a pusillanimous and insensitive spirit.

"Given the designated limits, I have taken the rem 'rock album' to mean an organic, structured creation which, like Shelley's idea of poetry, 'lifts the veil from the hidden beauty of the world and makes familiar objects be as if they were not familiar'; and I have chosen albums, which celebrate the buddings and ripenings of rock music."

Robert Christgau

A senior editor of the *Village Voice*, Robert Christgau is responsible for all music reviewing and writes a monthly Consumer Guide that has been widely imitated.

1	**Exile on Main Street** (7)	Rolling Stones
2	**Layla And Other Assorted Love Songs** (15)	Derek and the Dominoes
3	**The Immortal Otis Redding** (33)	Otis Redding
4	**More Chuck Berry** (75)	Chuck Berry
5	**12 Songs** (95)	Randy Newman
6	**Moondance** (22)	Van Morrison
7	**The Velvet Underground** (191)	Velvet Underground
8	**Rubber Soul** (5)	Beatles
9	**The Rolling Stones Now**	Rolling Stones
10	**Wild Honey**	Beach Boys

"My criteria were playability, depth of expression, and avoidance of waste. There's not a bad cut on any of these albums, and almost all of them are good to great. The only one I don't still play often is **12 Songs**, because it's not a casual kind of record.

"I decided not to 'vote' in this poll, but to rely on the records I've liked best over the years. I know everybody who votes for Chuck Berry is going to vote for **Golden Decade**, but I've always preferred **More**, which includes 'Come On' and 'Let It Rock' and avoids dubious (if pleasant) novelties like 'Too Pooped To Pop' and 'Anthony Boy'. Likewise, **The Best Of Otis Redding**, a remarkably well-constructed anthology, is a more obvious choice than **Immortal**, but **Immortal** happens to be a record I've played obsessively for almost a decade. If I'd followed this logic I might have selected **Something New**, one of six or seven Beatles albums that was in the running, but a final comparison with **Rubber Soul** (never an emotional favourite) was decisive. (I don't own the British versions of the Beatles LPs, but I love the **Rubber Soul** outtakes on **Yesterday — and Today**, which was also a contributing factor. **Yesterday — and Today** was in the running itself.) **Wild Honey** vs. **Endless Summer** was also this sort of problem.

"I think it's interesting that three of my six favourite albums came out in 1970 and that my favourite is also the most recent on my list. I haven't been listening much to Steely Dan lately or they would probably have made it, **Pretzel Logic** most likely; I also wonder about Al Green's horribly underrated **Call Me**. Too bad Motown never made good albums (Marvin Gaye's **Super Hits** was the only one with a shot). With a few years more perspective I might find a place for Eno's **Another Green World**, which I've been playing twice a week or so since it came out; I might also vote for one of the New York Dolls albums, which function in my life the way Randy Newman does — indispensably rich and evocative music for certain moments. And who knows how much I'll end up liking Television's **Marquee Moon**, which I'm OD'd on at the moment; I haven't been so enthusiastic about a new record in a very long time.

"One more thing — if I were making a list of my favourite albums, they wouldn't all be rock, not by a long shot. Duke Ellington's **Flaming Youth** (deleted, on RCA Vintage) would make it for sure; also, I think, Thelonious Monk and Charlie Parker."

Cameron Crowe

A freelance writer and Contributing Editor of *Rolling Stone*, Cameron Crowe became identified with a kind of subject (West Coast adult-orientated radio favourites) like some journalists become identified with a kind of style. He will turn 21 when the late Jack Benny turns 40.

1	After the Goldrush (40)	Neil Young and Crazy Horse
2	Rubber Soul (5)	Beatles
3	Jackson Browne (103)	Jackson Browne
4	Who's Next (19)	Who
5	Crosby, Stills and Nash (143)	Crosby, Stills and Nash
6	Let It Bleed (8)	Rolling Stones
7	For the Roses (142)	Joni Mitchell
8	Led Zeppelin (121)	Led Zeppelin
9	Desperado / Dixie Chicken	Eagles / Little Feat
10	Something/Anything	Todd Rundgren

Eve Dadomo

Giovanni Dadomo

A regular contributor to *Sounds*, *Time Out* and *Zigzag*, Giovanni Dadomo recorded with the Snivelling Shits in late 1977.

1	The Clash (24)	The Clash
2	1969 Velvet Underground Live (30)	Velvet Underground
3	Exile on Main Street (7)	Rolling Stones
4	Jonathan Richman and the Modern Lovers (131)	
5	My Generation (31)	Who
6	King of the Delta Blues Singers (182)	Robert Johnson
7	Golden Hour	Kinks
8	Da Capo	Love
9	The Sun Collection (11)	Elvis Presley
10	A Wizard, a True Star	Todd Rundgren

Robin Denselow

Rock and folk critic and feature writer for the *Guardian*, Robin

THE ROCK CRITICS & DJ'S

Denselow is also a producer of current affairs programmes for BBC Television.

1. **Abbey Road** (9) — Beatles
2. **Saint Dominic's Preview** (48) — Van Morrison
3. **Live at Leeds** (52) — Who
4. **Born to Run** (10) — Bruce Springsteen
5. **The Sun Collection** (11) — Elvis Presley
6. **Late for the Sky** (151) — Jackson Browne
7. **Ommadawn** (72) — Mike Oldfield
8. **Bringing It All Back Home** (27) — Bob Dylan
9. **Ummagumma** — Pink Floyd
10. **California Bloodlines** (36) — John Stewart

"Stewart is appallingly under-recognised, has made a string of great albums, and deserves to be praised by everyone from the country to the singer-songwriter fields. One of the great, poetic enthusiasts of Americana."

self-portrait

Chet Flippo

An associate editor of *Rolling Stone* in the New York office, Chet Flippo is a human crossover from country to pop.

1. **Legend** (20) — Buddy Holly
2. **Astral Weeks** (4) — Van Morrison
3. **Abbey Road** (9) — Beatles
4. **Blonde on Blonde** (2) — Bob Dylan
5. **My Generation** (31) — Who
6. **Out of Our Heads** (35) — Rolling Stones
7. **Truth** — Jeff Beck
8. **Allman Brothers Band at Fillmore East** (104) — Allman Brothers Band
9. **Layla And Other Assorted Love Songs** (15) — Derek and the Dominoes
10. **Born to Run** (10) — Bruce Springsteen

"Chuck Berry should have been there, too, but these are albums that I still play constantly. **Hot Rocks** is a terrific LP, but the impact of **Out of Our Heads** with 'Satisfaction' nosed it out. Rod Stewart is technically there since he was Beck's lead singer. The Beach Boys aren't even close. And what do we do about Robert Johnson?"

Ben Fong-Torres

One of the redwoods at *Rolling Stone* and now Senior Editor as well as writer of the magazine, Ben Fong-Torres broadcasts on KSAN-FM in San Francisco and recently scripted a national music awards programme.

1. **Sell Out** (69) — Who
2. **Rubber Soul** (5) — Beatles
3. **Boz Scaggs** (57) — Boz Scaggs
4. **Something Else** (118) — Kinks
5. **Joe Cocker!** (145) — Joe Cocker
6. **Moondance** (22) — Van Morrison
7. **Greatest Hits** (198) — Temptations
8. **December's Children** — Rolling Stones
9. **Dusty in Memphis** (160) — Dusty Springfield
10. **Phoebe Snow** — Phoebe Snow

Tom Sheehan

Pete Frame

A surveyor by current occupation, Pete Frame's pastime is charting the genealogy of rock acts. His tree diagrams have graced many an album sleeve and many issues of *Zigzag*, a magazine he wrote for and edited for many years.

1. **Astral Weeks** (4) — Van Morrison
2. **Blonde on Blonde** (2) — Bob Dylan
3. **California Bloodlines** (36) — John Stewart
4. **Wolfking of L.A.** (129) — John Phillips
5. **Notorious Byrd Brothers** (154) — Byrds
6. **Grievous Angel** (180) — Gram Parsons with Emmylou Harris
7. **Romance is on the Rise** (98) — Genevieve Waite
8. **First Album** — Holy Modal Rounders
9. **Golden Hits of the Shangri-Las** — Shangri-Las
10. **Old Number One** — Guy Clark

THE ROCK CRITICS & DJ'S

Simon Frith

An expert on singles whose reviews and essays have appeared in numerous publications and the *Rock File* series, Simon Frith has recently been a columnist for *Creem*.

1. **Highway 61 Revisited** (3)
   Bob Dylan
2. **Beggars Banquet** (42)
   Rolling Stones
3. **Sergeant Pepper's Lonely Hearts Club Band** (1)
   Beatles
4. **My Generation** (31)
   Who
5. **The Rise and Fall of Ziggy Stardust** (47)
   David Bowie
6. **Rock 'n' Roll Animal** (173)
   Lou Reed
7. **Hot Rats** (158)
   Frank Zappa
8. **Horses** (181)
   Patti Smith
9. **Whatevershebringswesing**
   Kevin Ayers
10. **12 Songs** (95)
    Randy Newman

"I believe that most of the greatest rock music of all time has appeared on singles, but, on the other hand, I don't think that anthologies are real 'rock albums'. So I haven't included any."

Paul Gambaccini

The author of this book, Paul Gambaccini, has an opinion on almost everything.

1. **Revolver** (6)
   Beatles
2. **Bringing It All Back Home** (27)
   Bob Dylan
3. **California Bloodlines** (36)
   John Stewart
4. **Sergeant Pepper's Lonely Hearts Club Band** (1)
   Beatles
5. **There Goes Rhymin' Simon** (44)
   Paul Simon
6. **Otis Blue** (23)
   Otis Redding
7. **Tapestry** (21)
   Carole King
8. **Going to a Go-Go** (97)
   Miracles
9. **Blood on the Tracks** (25)
   Bob Dylan
10. **The Spinners**
    The Spinners

"Producer Thom Bell is one of my ten all-time idols in this business, and **The Spinners** (UK title: **The Detroit Spinners**) is his masterpiece."

Charlie Gillett

The host of BBC Radio London's 'Honky Tonk', Charlie Gillett has written *Sound of the City* and *Making Tracks*, edited the *Rock File* series, co-directed Oval Records, and distinguished himself with contributions to *Rolling Stone* and the British pop music papers. He is currently re-writing *Sound of the City*.

1. **The Harder They Come** (26)
   Soundtrack from the Film
2. **Moondance** (22)
   Van Morrison
3. **Paradise and Lunch** (109)
   Ry Cooder
4. **Legend** (20)
   Buddy Holly
5. **Motown Songbook — The Original Versions** (140)
   Various Artists
6. **Sun Collection** (11)
   Elvis Presley
7. **Solid Gold Soul** (195)
   Various Artists
8. **Stacked Deck**
   Amazing Rhythm Aces
9. **Home Plate**
   Bonnie Raitt
10. **Howlin' Wind**
    Graham Parker and the Rumour

Bob Harris

Long the presenter of BBC 2's 'Old Grey Whistle Test', Bob Harris broadcasts on Thames Valley Radio and writes about rock. He spent a good deal of 1977 preparing a television film on Queen.

1. **Forever Changes** (16)
   Love
2. **Surf's Up** (54)
   Beach Boys
3. **Astral Weeks** (4)
   Van Morrison

THE ROCK CRITICS & DJ'S

4 Abbey Road (9)
Beatles

5 Playback (159)
Appletree Theatre

6 Fly Like an Eagle (171)
Steve Miller Band

7 Pet Sounds (12)
Beach Boys

8 Blonde on Blonde (2)
Bob Dylan

9 Music of My Mind
Stevie Wonder

10 H. P. Lovecraft 2
H. P. Lovecraft

"Totally subjective list, based on records that not only made a tremendous impact on me when they were first released, but have stayed with me since. **H.P. Lovecraft 2** and **Playback** are included because, like **Forever Changes**, they were some years ahead of their time, both in concept and performance."

Ron Jacobs

Recently a morning radio personality in his hometown of Honolulu, Hawaii, Ron Jacobs is known for one of the best programming minds in popular music radio. His greatest triumph was to build KHJ, Los Angeles, into a nationally important rock powerhouse.

1 Sergeant Pepper's Lonely Hearts Club Band (1)
Beatles

2 The Sun Collection (11)
Elvis Presley

3 Big Hits (High Tide and Green Grass) (37)
Rolling Stones

4 Blonde on Blonde (2)
Bob Dylan

5 American Beauty Rose (156)
Grateful Dead

6 Holland (185)
Beach Boys

7 Moondance (22)
Van Morrison

8 Dark Side of the Moon (135)
Pink Floyd

9 Greatest Hits
Simon and Garfunkel

10 Retrospective
Buffalo Springfield

Clive James

Australian by birth and sarcastic by character, wit and critic Clive James is known for his impersonation of Demis Roussos on the rock magazine programme 'So It Goes', his lyrics for Pete Atkin, his lengthy poem on the London critical fraternity, and his devastating comments about television and rock. He currently is television critic of *The Observer*.

1 Diana Ross And The Supremes' Greatest Hits (62)
Diana Ross & the Supremes

2 Legend (20)
Buddy Holly

3 Highway 61 Revisited (3)
Bob Dylan

4 The Beach Boy's Greatest Hits (115)
Beach Boys

5 Revolver (6)
Beatles

6 The Band (13)
The Band

7 Meaty, Beaty, Big and Bouncy (55)
Who

8 The Sun Collection (11)
Elvis Presley

9 Retrospective
Buffalo Springfield

10 Chuck Berry's Golden Decade (186)
Chuck Berry

"The Buffalo Springfield album is in because if it were out then a certain kind of power wouldn't be represented. In other words, I've tried to include all the different ways the music has appealed to me, but even then I've no room left for a dozen figures, ranging from Ry Cooder to Phil Spector, who have obsessed me at different times. And what about a perfect album like **Randy Newman Live** Most surprising omission – anything by the Rolling Stones. Never could stand them."

Kid Jensen

A Canadian by birth, Kid Jensen made a name for himself in Europe with 'Jensen's Dimensions' on Radio Luxembourg. He is heard regularly on BBC Radio 1 and seen presenting 'Top of the Pops' on BBC 1.

1 Astral Weeks (4)
Van Morrison

2 Are You Experienced? (17)
Jimi Hendrix Experience

3 What's Going On? (106)
Marvin Gaye

4 Hard Nose the Highway (77)
Van Morrison

5 Beggars' Banquet (42)
Rolling Stones

6 The Beatles (18)
Beatles

7 Otis Blue (23)
Otis Redding

THE ROCK CRITICS & DJ'S

Roberta Bayley

8. **Caravanserai** — Santana
9. **Songs to a Seagull** — Joni Mitchell
10. **Electric Music for the Mind and Body** — Country Joe and the Fish

"The Country Joe album opened my ears to sounds other than the mainstream top 40 of the day."

Murray The K

One of America's genuinely legendary disc jockeys, Murray 'the K' Kaufman has recently covered music and contemporary life style stories for Newsweek Broadcasting and served as a consultant for the Broadway musical 'Beatlemania'.

1. **Sergeant Pepper's Lonely Hearts Club Band** (1) — Beatles
2. **Talking Book** (92) — Stevie Wonder
3. **Bob Dylan Greatest Hits** (56) — Bob Dylan
4. **Hot Rocks 1964-1971** (90) — Rolling Stones
5. **Pet Sounds** (12) **Smiley Smile** — Beach Boys
6. **Parsley, Sage, Rosemary and Thyme** (34) — Simon and Garfunkel
7. **Mixed Bag** (200) — Richie Havens
8. **Mr. Tambourine Man / Turn Turn Turn** — Byrds
9. **Child Is Father to the Man** — Blood, Sweat and Tears
10. **Blonde on Blonde** (2) — Bob Dylan / **Tommy** (32) — Who

Lenny Kaye

The guitarist with the Patti Smith Group, Lenny Kaye is an associate editor of *Rock Scene* and an occasional rock journalist. He co-authored *Rock 100* and compiled the classic album **Nuggets**.

1. **Blonde on Blonde** (2) — Bob Dylan
2. **1969 Velvet Underground Live** (30) — Velvet Underground
3. **Funhouse** (114) — Stooges
4. **Johnny Burnette and His Rock 'n' Roll Trio** (136) — Johnny Burnette
5. **The Doors** (43) — The Doors
6. **Layla And Other Assorted Love Songs** (15) — Derek and the Dominoes
7. **I Dig Acapella Vol. 1** — Various Artists
8. **The Ronettes sing their Greatest Hits!** (78) — Ronettes featuring Veronica
9. **Electric Ladyland** (93) — Jimi Hendrix Experience
10. **Love and Peace** — Dadawah

*"This leaves out so much I'm embarrassed. Can you discount incredible careers (Beatles, Stones) for an oddball favourite? For the last, you can substitute (how about the Who?) anything by the Beach Boys, Grateful Dead, Elvis (especially **The Sun Collection**), Yardbirds, Miracles, or eight million oldies collections."*

Dave Laing

A prolific rock author, critic and editor in the early and mid-1970s, Dave Laing is preparing a history of the record industry while continuing to write reviews.

1. **The Beatles 1962-66** (38) — Beatles
2. **Direct Hits** (86) — Who
3. **Imagine** (28) — John Lennon
4. **I Want to See the Bright Lights Tonight** (133) — Richard and Linda Thompson
5. **Blues Breakers** (152) — John Mayall and Eric Clapton
6. **Hunky Dory** (170) — David Bowie
7. **Dusty in Memphis** (160) — Dusty Springfield
8. **Dark Side of the Moon** (135) — Pink Floyd
9. **Fog on the Tyne** — Lindesfarne
10. **Bleach** — Raymond Froggatt

"To choose just ten of all rock albums is too daunting, so I've limited myself to British artists, particularly those grappling with the paradox of working with an American music to express a non-American experience, e.g. (4), (9), and (10). Froggatt starts from Dylan and working class Birmingham and comes up with supremely relevant rock and roll."

THE ROCK CRITICS & DJ'S

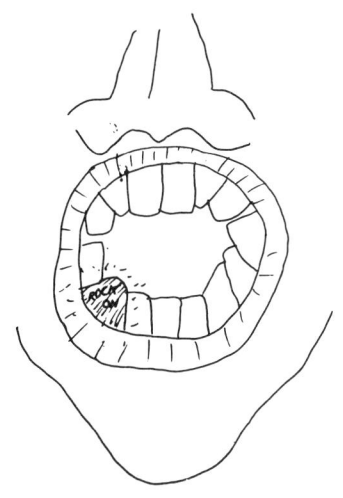

self-portrait

Greil Marcus

The book critic for *Rolling Stone*, Greil Marcus is the author of *Mystery Train: Images of America in Rock 'n' Roll Music*. He has been one of the most distinguished rock critics to go between hard covers.

1. **Let It Bleed** (8)
   Rolling Stones
2. **Highway 61 Revisited** (3)
   Bob Dylan
3. **Every Picture Tells a Story** (46)
   Rod Stewart
4. **Astral Weeks** (4)
   Van Morrison
5. **With the Beatles** (50)
   Beatles
6. **Exile on Main Street** (7)
   Rolling Stones
7. **Rubber Soul** (USA version) (5)
   Beatles
8. **More Chuck Berry** (75)
   Chuck Berry
9. **Elvis' Golden Records** (116)
   Elvis Presley
10. **Little Richard's 17 Grooviest Original Hits**
    Little Richard

"**Let It Bleed** is not only one of the most intelligent rock and roll albums ever made, but also one of the most visceral and exciting. It not only summed up its era as well as any recording has ever done, it has escaped its era, and sounds as direct and mysterious today as it did upon release in late 1969. It includes what may well be the greatest single rock and roll performance ('Gimme Shelter') plus some of the most surprising ('You Got the Silver', 'You Can't Always Get What You Want'). **Let It Bleed** is more than anyone could have expected from the Rolling Stones – more, in fact, than any fan could have hoped for. That kind of satisfaction is part of what rock and roll is all about.

"The other selections above are not arbitrary, but aside from **Let It Bleed**, the rankings are. Modern albums are listed higher than classic rock collections simply because they are albums, not collections. Such a listing cannot, of course, say anything much about rock and roll as such; that would take a list of singles and album cuts, with room for at least one hundred entries. A list that must omit Sam Cooke's 'A Change is Gonna Come' or 'The Five Satins', 'In the Still of the Night' or everything by Phil Spector and Motown is an almost private conceit. Still, here we find something of the very best, and in several cases, albums that contain tracks that can honestly be put forward as the greatest rock and roll of all: Rod Stewart's 'Every Picture Tells a Story', the Beatles' 'Money' (from **With the Beatles**), 'Gimme Shelter' by the Rolling Stones, Chuck Berry's 'Johnny B. Goode', Little Richard's 'Tutti Frutti', Elvis' 'Milkcow Blues Boogie' (**A Date with Elvis**) or 'Hound Dog' (**Golden Hits**), and Bob Dylan's titanic 'Like a Rolling Stone'.

"It is surprising, too, how many of the very greatest single instrumental performances in the history of rock and roll turn up on a list of ten 12-inch LPs. The ultimate in rock and roll drumming is Mick Waller's cataclysmic assault on 'Every Picture Tells a Story' (runners-up: Kenneth Buttrey on Bob Dylan's 'Absolutely Sweet Marie', from **Blonde on Blonde**; Hal Blaine on the Phil Spector/Ronettes 'Be My Baby'). The finest bass playing in all of rock is that of Richard Davis on **Astral Weeks** (runners-up: James Jamerson on any number of Motown classics; Charlie McCoy on Dylan's **John Wesley Harding**). Rhythm guitar is a toss-up between Elvis on 'Mystery Train', Bob Dylan on 'Like a Rolling Stone', and – my choice – Martin Quittenton on 'Every Picture Tells a Story' (note that both Elvis and Quittenton played acoustic, not electric). My sentimental favourite for piano would be the unknown genius (Carole King?) on the Chiffons' 'One Fine Day', though I would settle for Lafayette Leake's magnificent work on 'Johnny B. Goode'. Harmonica belongs to Bob Dylan alone, for 'Absolutely Sweet Marie'; saxophone to Boots Randolph on Elvis 'Reconsider Baby' (from **Elvis is Back**). And lead guitar – well, it is either Chuck, on 'Johnny B. Goode', or Keith Richard, following Berry's lines, in 'Gimme Shelter'.

"Not that rock is made up of virtuoso solo performances; it is no accident that more than one tune cited contains more than one of the supreme performances, and that neither 'Money' nor 'Tutti Frutti' can be broken down into its parts. Rock is a continuum: my list represents only a few explosions, albeit those whose echo can still be heard, explosions that will be audible as long as anyone is listening."

Dave Marsh

A guiding light of the early Creem, Dave Marsh went on to become Records editor of

THE ROCK CRITICS & DJ'S

Rolling Stone. With the semi-retirement of Jon Landau he became the rock critic most likely to be asked to appear on a television panel or name-dropped in a magazine column.

1. **Born to Run** (10)
   Bruce Springsteen
2. **A Date with Elvis** (74)
   Elvis Presley
3. **Let It Bleed** (8)
   Rolling Stones
4. **Highway 61 Revisited** (3)
   Bob Dylan
5. **Who's Next** (19)
   Who
6. **Abbey Road** (9)
   Beatles
7. **Layla And Other Assorted Love Songs** (15)
   Derek and the Dominoes
8. **Are You Experienced?** (17)
   Jimi Hendrix Experience
9. **Every Picture Tells a Story** (46)
   Rod Stewart
10. **A Christmas Gift For You From Philles Records** (later known as **Phil Spector's Christmas Album**)

Bruce Morrow

A long-term fixture on New York evening radio as 'Cousin Brucie', Bruce Morrow is writing an autobiographical account on the AM world in which he starred and the creeping automation which led him to leave it.

1. **Endless Summer** (39)
   Beach Boys
2. **All Things Must Pass** (79)
   George Harrison
3. **Tapestry** (21)
   Carole King
4. **Sergeant Pepper's Lonely Hearts Club Band** (1)
   Beatles
5. **Woodstock** (150)
   Various Artists
6. **Songs in the Key of Life** (41)
   Stevie Wonder
7. **Highway 61 Revisited** (3)
   Bob Dylan
8. **Parsley, Sage, Rosemary and Thyme** (34)
   Simon and Garfunkel
9. **Hair**
   Original Cast
10. **Deja Vu**
    Crosby, Stills, Nash and Young

"I have selected my top ten albums as I feel they all represent and have influenced a musical style and era. They have all stimulated and participated in sociological change."

Hervé Muller

The producer of an FM rock programme in France, Hervé Muller writes mostly for the French magazine *Rock and Folk* and the daily *Le Matin de Paris*. He is an occasional photographer and concert promoter.

1. **Sticky Fingers** (68)
   Rolling Stones
2. **Absolutely Live** (80)
   Doors
3. **Highway 61 Revisited** (3)
   Bob Dylan
4. **White Light/White Heat** (125)
   Velvet Underground
5. **The Harder They Come** (26)
   Soundtrack from the Film
6. **The Soft Machine** (177)
   Soft Machine
7. **Are You Experienced?** (17)
   Jimi Hendrix Experience
8. **Disraeli Gears**
   Cream
9. **GP**
   Gram Parsons
10. **Tonight's the Night**
    Neil Young

"Nothing very unusual there, except the first Soft Machine (certainly the most overlooked album of all time!) and **The Harder They Come** (reggae being the best thing that happened to rock in the seventies; this is a near-perfect reggae collection). I'm not especially a Neil Young fan, but **Tonight** blew my mind as being the heaviest and one of the most real recording(s) ever made. Quite scary, in fact. Since then Mr Young went back on his Californian tracks, but there was no way he could have made another album like that.

"Gram Parsons is for me one of the most important figures of the American rock and country scene, and was better than ever at the end, that's why I decided on **GP** rather than the first Flyin' Burrito LP.

"The Doors' one is certainly the best live album of all time, that's why I picked that one rather than **L.A. Woman** or **The Doors**.

"What's a 'greatest rock album' anyway? The order of preference is even more arbitrary, it's all a question of mood. The Stooges' first, **Wailers Live**, Clapton's **Leyla**, Jackie Lomax' **3**, Lynyrd Skynyrd, among others should/could have been there, and after I mail this I'll probably remember the one album I shouldn't have forgotten."

Scott Muni

The Programme Director of WNEW-FM in New York, Scott

THE ROCK CRITICS & DJ'S

Muni is on the air every weekday between 2 and 6 p.m. He is also fondly remembered in the City for his early work on WMCA and WABC.

1. **Parsley, Sage, Rosemary and Thyme** (34) — Simon and Garfunkel
2. **The Beatles** (18) — Beatles
3. **Magical Mystery Tour** (138) — Beatles
4. **Sergeant Pepper's Lonely Hearts Club Band** (1) — Beatles
5. **Works, Vol. 1** (157) — Emerson, Lake and Palmer
6. **Frampton Comes Alive** (49) — Peter Frampton
7. **Bob Dylan Greatest Hits** (56) / **Bob Dylan Greatest Hits Vol. 2** — Bob Dylan
8. **Tea for the Tillerman** — Cat Stevens
9. **Did She Mention My Name? / Greatest Hits** — Gordon Lightfoot
10. **Hot Rocks 1964-1971** (90) / **More Hot Rocks** — Rolling Stones

Anne Nightingale

Britain's foremost female disc jockey, Anne Nightingale came to the attention of radio and television producers through her rock journalism of the sixties. It is she Eric Clapton is kissing in the gatefold of **Slowhand**. She currently presents 'Anne Nightingale's Request Show' Sunday afternoons on BBC Radio 1 and writes for *Cosmopolitan* and *The Daily Express*.

1. **In the Court of the Crimson King** (65) — King Crimson
2. **Sergeant Pepper's Lonely Hearts Club Band** (1) — Beatles
3. **Who's Next** (19) — Who
4. **461 Ocean Boulevard** (124) — Eric Clapton
5. **The Rise and Fall of Ziggy Stardust** (47) — David Bowie
6. **Pet Sounds** (12) — Beach Boys
7. **Mythical Kings and Iguanas** — Dory Previn
8. **Blood on the Tracks** (25) — Bob Dylan
9. **The Royal Scam** — Steely Dan
10. **Paris 1919** (155) — John Cale

Mark P

The founder of *Sniffin' Glue*, punk's premier fanzine, Mark P. is a freelance writer and member of the group Alternative T.V.

1. **The Clash** (24) — The Clash
2. **We're Only In It for the Money** (53) — Mothers of Invention
3. **Ramones** (112) — Ramones
4. **Catch a Fire** (126) — Wailers
5. **Electric Warrior** (162) — T. Rex
6. **Ege Bamyasi** (184) — Can
7. **New York Dolls** (199) — New York Dolls
8. **Quadrophenia** — Who
9. **Unlimited Edition** — Can
10. **CB Zoo** — Dillinger

"Perhaps all of my list is unusual, but I must listen to honesty rather than 'great rock albums'. Reggae's in the list 'cause I think it's better than 'rock'. T. Rex are funny."

Tony Palmer

The brains behind the television series and best-selling book *All You Need Is Love: The Story of Popular Music*, Tony Palmer was music critic for *The Observer* from 1966 to 1974. He broadcasts regularly on BBC Radio 4 and comes out with books and television documentaries on subjects ranging from the Oz trials to Liberace.

(Tony Palmer's top ten are not in order of preference.)

THE ROCK CRITICS & DJ'S

1. **Ommadawn** (72) — Mike Oldfield
2. **Revolver** (6) — Beatles
3. **Led Zeppelin IV** (29) — Led Zeppelin
4. **Imagine** (28) — John Lennon
5. **The Sun Collection** (11) — Elvis Presley
6. **Wish You Were Here** (146) — Pink Floyd
7. **Goodbye** (148) — Cream
8. **John Wesley Harding** (139) — Bob Dylan
9. **Joplin In Concert** (144) — Janis Joplin
10. **Electric Ladyland** (93) — Jimi Hendrix Experience

Tim Rice

The writer of 'Jesus Christ Superstar' and 'Evita', Tim Rice recently co-authored *The Guinness Book of British Hit Singles*. He may occasionally be heard broadcasting on almost every BBC network.

1. **Worldwide 50 Gold Award Hits, Vol. 1** (70) — Elvis Presley
2. **Big Hits (High Tide and Green Grass)** (37) — Rolling Stones
3. **The Buddy Holly Story** (100) — Buddy Holly
4. **With the Beatles** (52) — Beatles
5. **Cosmo's Factory** (96) — Creedence Clearwater Revival
6. **Bridge Over Troubled Water** (168) — Simon and Garfunkel
7. **Cliff's Hit Album** (188) — Cliff Richard and the Shadows
8. **The Fabulous Style of the Everly Brothers** — Everly Brothers
9. **Highway 61 Revisited** (3) — Bob Dylan
10. **Doors 13** — Doors
    Hats Off to Del Shannon — Del Shannon

Lisa Robinson

The Hedda Hopper, Louella Parsons *and* Rona Barrett of the New York rock set, Lisa Robinson is a syndicated columnist, editor of *Hit Parader*, and associate editor of *Rock Scene, Creem* and the *New Musical Express*.

1. **The Velvet Underground and Nico** (14)
2. **The Beatles** (18) — Beatles
3. **Exile on Main Street** (7) — Rolling Stones
4. **Blonde on Blonde** (2) — Bob Dylan
5. **Chelsea Girl** (149) — Nico
6. **Paris 1919** (155) — John Cale
7. **Romance is on the Rise** (98) — Genevieve Waite
8. **Marquee Moon** — Television
9. **Horses** (181) — Patti Smith
10. **Elvis Presley** — Elvis Presley

"These are the records I play the most. It was hard picking **Exile** over **Flowers** and **Between the Buttons** which I used to love, but I think if I was on a desert island now, I'd take **Exile.** Same situation with picking **Blonde on Blonde** over **Highway 61 Revisited.** *The Elvis LP was the first album I ever had, and I loved it so much that even though I don't listen to it now, I had to include it. I wish there was room for the Stooges' first and for Derek and the Dominoes'* **Layla** . . ."

Gabrielle Goodchild

Robert Shelton

A reviewer for the London *Times* and a stringer for *Time*, Robert Shelton has authored several books on pop music and is putting finishing touches on his definitive work on Bob Dylan. His historic *New York Times* review of an early Dylan performance is reproduced on the sleeve of the debut album **Bob Dylan**.

1. **Blonde on Blonde** (2) — Bob Dylan
2. **Out of Our Heads** (35) — Rolling Stones
3. **Aretha: Ten Years of Gold** (102) — Aretha Franklin
4. **Highway 61 Revisited** (3) — Bob Dylan
5. **Cheap Thrills** (76) — Big Brother and the Holding Company
6. **Blood on the Tracks** (25) — Bob Dylan
7. **Physical Graffiti** (192) — Led Zeppelin
8. **Chuck Berry's Golden Decade** (186) — Chuck Berry

THE ROCK CRITICS & DJ'S

9 Hard Nose the Highway (77)
Van Morrison

10 Dock of the Bay
Otis Redding

"Clearly a partisan list by a critic who dislikes lists and charts. Dylan, black singers and women have shaped rock enormously. They keep it fresh, alive and mature. All here have cast giant shadows even as they've spread the light."

Dick Summer

The success of his late night blend of music and readings on WBZ in the late sixties led Dick Summer to publish several volumes. He recently had a disc jockey stint on WNBC.

1 Revolver (6)
Beatles

2 Surrealistic Pillow (73)
Jefferson Airplane

3 Tapestry (21)
Carole King

4 Sergeant Pepper's Lonely Hearts Club Band (1)
Beatles

5 Rubber Soul (5)
Beatles

6 Album 1700 (179)
Peter, Paul and Mary

7 Blood, Sweat and Tears (50)
Blood, Sweat and Tears

8 Parsley, Sage, Rosemary and Thyme (34)
Simon and Garfunkel

9 Hot Buttered Soul
Isaac Hayes

10 Tommy (32)
Who

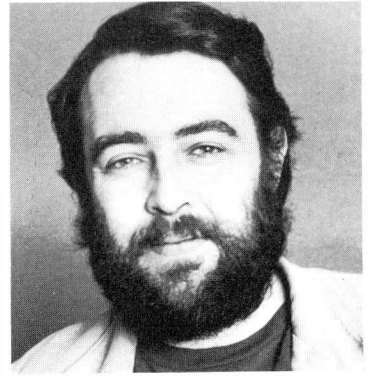

John Tobler

A regular contributor to BBC Radio 1's 'Rock On,' John Tobler has for years been an integral part of *Zigzag* magazine. He has authored several books on rock.

1 And the Hits Just Keep On Comin' (58)
Michael Nesmith

2 The Doors (43)
The Doors

3 Sailor (105)
Steve Miller Band

4 Sergeant Pepper's Lonely Hearts Club Band (1)
Beatles

5 Blonde on Blonde (2)
Bob Dylan

6 Otis Blue (23)
Otis Redding

7 Saint Dominic's Preview (48)
Van Morrison

8 Boz Scaggs (57)
Boz Scaggs

9 Who Knows Where the Time Goes?
Judy Collins

10 Late for the Sky (151)
Jackson Browne

"The Doors' choice could just as easily have been Strange Days or Waiting for the Sun, while several other Van Morrison LPs were possible inclusions. The Judy Collins album contains what I feel is the ultimate supergroup playing on 'Someday Soon' — James Burton, Stephen Stills, Van Dyke Parks, Buddy Emmons and Jim Gordon.'

Don Topping

Known as 'El Numero Uno,' Don Topping is afternoon drive time disc jockey at RJR Kingston, Jamaica.

Tom Sheehan

1 Stand (67)
Sly and the Family Stone

2 Blood, Sweat and Tears (51)
Blood, Sweat and Tears

3 Abbey Road (9)
Beatles

4 With a Little Help From My Friends (128)
Joe Cocker

5 Live at Carnegie Hall (147)
Chicago

6 Are You Experienced? (17)
Jimi Hendrix Experience

7 That's the Way of the World
Earth Wind and Fire

8 Bitches' Brew
Miles Davis

9 Jesus Christ Superstar
Original Recording

10 They Only Come Out at Night
Edgar Winter Group

"Bitches' Brew was one of the first really great albums fully utilizing the jazz-rock fusion. Jesus Christ Superstar was a significant innovation that paid dividends."

Rosalie Trombley

The long-time Music Director of CKLW, a radio station transmitting from Windsor, Ontario, but thinking Detroit, Rosalie Trombley has broken more important hits and artists than any other AM MD. Bob Seger immortalized her in 'Rosalie.'

THE ROCK CRITICS & DJ'S

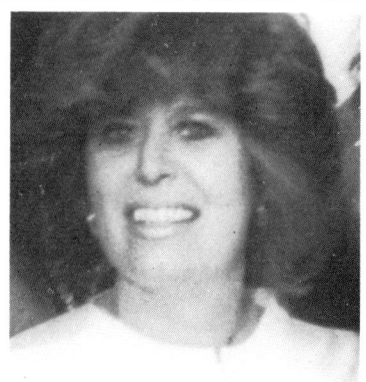

Penny Valentine

After rising to fame as a top pop journalist in London in the Swinging Sixties, Penny Valentine left home base to work for record companies in the early seventies. She is now safely at home freelancing.

1. **Songs in the Key of Life** (41)
   Stevie Wonder
2. **Live Bullet** (87)
   Bob Seger & The Silver Bullet Band
3. **Frampton Comes Alive** (49)
   Peter Frampton
4. **Goodbye Yellow Brick Road** (122)
   Elton John
5. **Their Greatest Hits 1971-75** (141)
   Eagles
6. **Endless Summer** (39)
   Beach Boys
7. **Chicago IX (Greatest Hits)** (193)
   Chicago
8. **The Beatles 1962-1966** (38)
   The Beatles 1967-1970 (163)
   Beatles
9. **Led Zeppelin IV** (29)
   Led Zeppelin
10. **Meaty Beaty Big and Bouncy** (55)
    Who

Ed Ward

A freelance writer for numerous American magazines, Ed Ward also does freelance editorial work. It was Ed who as Reviews Editor of *Rolling Stone* in 1970 accepted an unsolicited manuscript from the author of this book, setting in motion a curious career.

1. **Forever Changes** (41)
   Love
2. **The Band** (13)
   The Band
3. **American Gothic** (110)
   David Ackles
4. **Highway 61 Revisited** (3)
   Bob Dylan
5. **Who's Next** (19)
   Who
6. **Greetings From Asbury Park N.J.** (169)
   Bruce Springsteen
7. **Live at Monterey** (189)
   Otis Redding/The Jimi Hendrix Experience
8. **Surf's Up** (53)
   Beach Boys
9. **Elton John**
   Elton John
10. **Anthology**
    Gladys Knight and the Pips

1. **Dedicated to You** (61)
   Five Royales
2. **Between the Buttons** (83)
   Rolling Stones
3. **Blonde on Blonde** (2)
   Bob Dylan
4. **Revolver** (6)
   Beatles
5. **Cigars, Candy, Acapella** (161)
   Belmonts
6. **Mendocino** (183)
   Sir Douglas Quintet
7. **Taking Tiger Mountain** (194)
   Eno
8. **Kink Kontroversy**
   Kinks
9. **1969 Velvet Underground Live** (30)
   Velvet Underground
10. **Hoboken Saturday Night**
    Insect Trust

"The Belmonts' album epitomizes the street corner singing and group harmonizing I grew up with. Sir Doug combined melody, innocence and an unselfconscious feeling to the demo tapes that wound up as **Mendocino**. Eno proves there still are 'progressive' things to be done with a rock context in a time of increasing formularization and sterility. The Velvets express my home town, New York, better than anybody ever did. And the Insect Trust was a great idea that never really came into being as a live act, but on record they managed to combine everything that's good about American popular music."

Chuck Krall

Chris Welch

The features editor of *Melody Maker*, Chris Welch is also known for his anonymous appearances in The Raver, his book on Jimi Hendrix, and his occasional unheralded outings as a musician.

1. **Sergeant Pepper's Lonely Hearts Club Band** (1)
   Beatles
2. **Led Zeppelin II** (88)
   Led Zeppelin

THE ROCK CRITICS & DJ'S

3. **Pet Sounds** (12) — Beach Boys
4. **Axis: Bold as Love** (123) — Jimi Hendrix Experience
5. **Live at Leeds** (52) — Who
6. **Forever Changes** (16) — Love
7. **Sound of '65** (196) — Graham Bond
8. **We're Only In It for the Money** (53) — Mothers of Invention
9. **Hot Rats** (158) — Frank Zappa
10. **Skip Bifferty** — Skip Bifferty

"Only one album was released by Skip Bifferty, the group that featured Graham Bell as lead singer. The group were wracked by business problems, and plagued by temperament, but they produced one interesting, promising album, containing fey, wayward, stoned songs that were intriguing and appealing. John Peel was one of their greatest fans. No more need be said.

"Graham Bond was an underrated pioneer who helped in the ground work for both the jazz-rock scene (before Miles Davis, please note) and the heavy bands of the later sixties."

Joel Whitburn

The most complete researcher rock music has ever known, Joel Whitburn is the compiler and publisher of the Record Researcher series of books tabulating the *Billboard* Pop, LP, Rhythm and Blues, Country and Western and Easy Listening charts. His works were the direct inspiration for the quartet who compiled *The Guinness Book of British Hit Singles*.

1. **Sergeant Pepper's Lonely Hearts Club Band** (1) — Beatles
2. **Captain Fantastic and the Brown Dirt Cowboy** (85) — Elton John
3. **Days of Future Passed** (107) — Moody Blues
4. **The Beatles** (18) — The Beatles
5. **Led Zeppelin IV** (29) — Led Zeppelin
6. **Tommy** (32) — Who
7. **One of These Nights** (190) — Eagles
8. **Machine Head** — Deep Purple
9. **Cosmo's Factory** (96) — Creedence Clearwater Revival
10. **A Night at the Opera** — Queen

"Not counting greatest hits albums, the above list contains some of the greatest original listening of rock tunes that one could ever want. It certainly is tough to leave out some of the creative artists and 'genius' albums like Bob Dylan, Stevie Wonder, Rolling Stones, Jimi Hendrix, Chicago, Pink Floyd, **Wheels of Fire, Beatles VI, The Doors, In-A-Gadda-Da-Vida,** and so many, many more."

Ellen Willis

A Contributing Editor of *Rolling Stone*, Ellen Willis is also a staff writer for the *New Yorker*.

1. **Let It Bleed** (8) — Rolling Stones
2. **Highway 61 Revisited** (3) — Bob Dylan
3. **The Band** (13) — The Band
4. **Golden Archive Series** (127) — Velvet Underground
5. **Tommy** (32) — Who
6. **Otis Redding in Europe** (167) — Otis Redding
7. **The Beatles' Second Album** — Beatles
8. **Out of Our Heads** (35) — Rolling Stones
9. **Chuck Berry's Golden Hits** — Chuck Berry
10. **Cheap Thrills** (76) — Big Brother and the Holding Company

Richard Williams

The editor of *Time Out*, Richard Williams has often written for *The Times* and *Melody Maker*.

1. **Pet Sounds** (12) — Beach Boys
2. **In 1966 There Was . . .** (89) — Bob Dylan and The Band Live at the Albert Hall
3. **Otis Blue** (23) — Otis Redding
4. **Rubber Soul** (5) — Beatles
5. **The Velvet Underground and Nico** (14)
6. **Going to a Go-Go** (97) — Miracles
7. **Back in the USA** (71) — MC5

THE ROCK CRITICS & DJ'S

8 James Brown at the Apollo, Vol. 1 (45)
James Brown

9 Standing Ovation
Gladys Knight and the Pips

10 The Royal Scam
Steely Dan
The Hissing of Summer Lawns
Joni Mitchell

"I have attempted to choose under two main criteria: (1) intrinsic merit; (2) personal enjoyment. However, I also tried to take into consideration the importance of each record to its time in both musical and social aspects.

"It is interesting to note that (in this field of musical endeavour, at least) the best usually manages to rise to the top. All but one of the artists and groups in my tabulation have achieved fame and absolute or relative wealth, which is both coincidental and gratifying."

Pete Wingfield

One of Britain's foremost experts on soul music and a freelance rock journalist, musician Pete Wingfield had an international hit of his own in his spare time with 'Eighteen With A Bullet.'

1 James Brown At The Apollo, Vol. 1 (45)
James Brown

2 Soul Dressing (91)
Booker T. and the M.G.s

3 Live at the Regal (111)
B. B. King

4 Rockin' Pneumonia and the Boogie Woogie Flu (134)
Huey 'Piano' Smith and the Clowns

5 The Ronettes Sing Their Greatest Hits! (78)
Ronettes featuring Veronica

6 Genius Sings the Blues (172)
Ray Charles

7 Everything is Everything (197)
Donny Hathaway

8 Amazing Grace
Aretha Franklin

9 Pet Sounds (12)
Beach Boys

10 The Band (13)
The Band

"Deciding what to omit was an agonizing process — main difficulty being that many worthy candidates (Motown acts, Philly Soul groups, doo wop names, Spector, and so on) didn't/don't make consistently good albums, being singles orientated acts. Lack of current stuff in my list doesn't mean that I don't think the music keeps on getting better and better — I've always maintained that it does! — but only that ability to stand the test of time seemed like a good criteria for inclusion in the list.

"Comments:
"Number 2. The second most worn album in my collection. At one time the group I played in at the time did hopefully imitative versions of virtually every track off **Soul Dressing**...
"Number 4. Well, it was a tie really between this and **Little Richard Vol. 2** in the 'New Orleans R&B' bracket. Chose this as being less well-known. Nobody since has equalled Huey & the Clowns hard-driving good vibes. (Guy Stevens' idea of the Breughel Painting for the cover was a good idea too).
"Number 7. I know he's not considered a major lasting talent, but this set — together with his 'live' album — just makes me jump and shout! What a shame he's apparently slipped into self-imposed oblivion.
"Number 8. Not Aretha's most celebrated work, but it shows her back at home in the church, and is every bit as electrifying as her late 60s soul hits.

"Number 9. This record was the chief reason I stopped being an R&B snob!
"Number 10. Obviously this group's finest achievement; all-American music that defies categories.
"Finally, can I nominate an 'honorary number 11' and cheat a bit by making it the entire 13 album **Oldies But Goodies** collection an original sound out of Hollywood — the definitive oldies set..."

Ritchie Yorke

Canada's best-known rock writer, Ritchie Yorke has recently authored *The History of Rock 'n' Roll*, *The Led Zeppelin Biography*, and *Into the Music: the Van Morrison Biography*.

1 Even in the Quietest Moments (63)
Supertramp

2 Astral Weeks (4)
Van Morrison

3 Crime of the Century (108)
Supertramp

4 In Concert with the Edmonton Symphony Orchestra (132)
Procul Harum

5 Lady Soul (81)
Aretha Franklin

6 Shoot Out at the Fantasy Factory (175)
Traffic

7 Led Zeppelin (121)
Led Zeppelin

8 Alone Together
Dave Mason

9 American Pie
Don McLean

10 Madman Across the Water
Elton John